WHERE THEY STOOD

.II.

WHERE THEY STOOD

The Evolution of the Black Anglo Community in Montreal

by

Researchers and Authors

Matthew Mullone

Sherwins Jean

Anne Victoria Jean-François

Jessica Williams-Daley

Renee White

Amanda Georgina Ghartey Asomani-Nyarko

Yoanna Joseph

Donna Fabiola Ingabire

Fanta Ly

BLACK COMMUNITY RESOURCE CENTRE

.ll.

Copyediting: Elise Moser, Kaiya Cade Smith Blackburn
Author photo: Marlena Goldberg
Cover image: Melis Karayusuf
Cover design: Leila Marshy, Debbie Geltner
Book design: DiTech

Library and Archives Canada Cataloguing in Publication

Title: Where they stood: the evolution of the Black Anglo community in Montreal / by researchers and authors working with Montreal's Black Community Resource Centre.
Identifiers: Canadiana (print) 20220436312 | Canadiana (ebook) 20220436460 | ISBN 9781773901343 (softcover) | ISBN 9781773901367 (PDF) | ISBN 9781773901350 (EPUB)
Subjects: LCSH: Canadians, English-speaking—Québec (Province)—Montréal—History. | CSH: Black Canadians—Québec—Montreal—History
Classification: LCC FC2947.9.B6 W52 2023 | DDC 971.4/2700496—dc23

Printed and bound in Canada by Imprimerie Gauvin.
Legal deposit – Library and Archives Canada and Bibliothèque et Archives nationales du Québec, 2023

The Black Community Resource Centre acknowledges the support of the Government of Canada for their project.
For references, sources, notes, links and credits compiled for *Where They Stood* by the Black Community Resource Centre and the authors, please see: http://www.bcrcmontreal.com.wheretheystood.com.

Linda Leith Publishing gratefully acknowledges the support of the Government of Canada through the Canada Council for the Arts and the Canada Book Fund and that of the Government of Quebec through the Société de développement des entreprises culturelles (SODEC) and the Programme de crédit d'impôt pour l'édition de livres—Gestion SODEC.

Linda Leith Publishing
Montreal
www.lindaleith.com

Table of Contents

Foreword

Sara DeMelo-Zare and Ayana Monuma

Montreal was a centre of Canadian immigration throughout the latter part of the 20th century. The city saw the arrival of migrants from all over the world and a considerable increase in the Black immigrant population beginning in the 1960s. Please see diagrams, pp. 182–184.

This influx was largely due to changes in Canadian immigration policies that allowed for greater Black migration. However, Canada remained highly racialized. Black Canadians faced discrimination and were disadvantaged both socially and economically. Black communities in Montreal, which is a predominantly white space, lacked the resources to mitigate these inequities.

The Black Community Resource Centre (BCRC) was created to address the overarching concerns of Montreal's Black populations. There were few Black spaces designed to provide social, economic, and academic support to the community. In 1992, the Val Morin Black Forum confirmed the need for a community-driven body to support Black residents, and the BCRC was formed as a result.

The BCRC continues to foster a comprehensive community-based approach to its programs and projects. Most notably, it supports established generations, while nurturing the next. This is crucial to ensuring the continuity of this small, interwoven community.

History is preserved through documentation, but also through tradition and access to memory. The knowledge of Black history enables understanding and compassion between peoples and is essential to a sustained sense of identity for Black communities. The wisdom and knowledge of community members are fundamental to the vitality of Black history. The only way our history is known is through the experiences and lives of our predecessors. Black youth can utilize these teachings as a means not only to combat widespread discrimination and xenophobia, but to promote inclusion, acceptance, and appreciation. By instilling that understanding in Black youth, our history is honoured and protected. We must encourage solidarity, community, belonging and identity as we continue to operate in a society engineered to erase individuality. Black youth are enthusiastic to know their history as are their elders.

Our idea emerged during a time of political unrest in the Western world. The words "Black Lives Matter" filled every television news ticker, website, and social media forum. But what did it all mean? Black people in North America were still being discriminated against, violently attacked, and *murdered* because of the colour of their skin.

George Floyd, an unarmed Black man, was murdered by police officer Derek Chauvin on May 25, 2020 in Minneapolis, MN. This death sparked a nationwide movement, with protests combatting police brutality and the use of excessive force forming the largest act of civic organizing in the United States since the Civil Rights era.

It is widely thought that Canada is immune to this level of prejudice, to this level of racism. However, no part of the Western world is exempt. Systemic racism has been present in Canada, and specifically Montreal, throughout its history.

The deaths of Anthony Griffin in 1987, Fredy Villanueva in 2008, and Nicholas Gibbs in 2018 generated discussions of racial profiling by Montreal's police force. The events confirmed that the city still had a systemic racism issue. Those meant to serve and protect were abusing their power in ways that were killing Black men. The officers involved in the three murders were never persecuted for their actions.

During times of anger, sadness, and volatility, we require understanding. And in this sociopolitical climate, we are in desperate need of humanity and change. *Where They Stood* is meant to bridge the gap between communities. We want people of all ethnic and social backgrounds discussing the Black experience. Respect and tolerance come from a place of knowledge. We offer our book to anyone who is willing to educate themselves.

We created *Where They Stood* to promote visibility, to popularize Black history beyond racism and slavery, and to highlight Black achievement. At a time of such injustice, we want to shine light on the activists, the labourers, the immigrants, all the people who forged the path for new generations to walk. This book is meant to share stories frequently neglected. We want to counter the negativity often put forth when discussing Black history, and focus on moments of joy, positivity, and triumph. *Where They Stood* looks to reimagine what possibilities lie ahead for the Black community.

Where They Stood was designed to be a collaborative project incorporating a diverse set of voices within a shared community. The team recruited Black English-speaking youth to author a book highlighting the important events and key figures that shaped Black Anglo Montreal. We found individuals who could bring forward their passion for the community—inspired by their personal experiences—to the project.

The youth who have authored this book have strong academic backgrounds and the necessary drive. We began as a group of strangers, and friendships blossomed over the course of this project. Educators and community members volunteered their time. With the help of these field professionals, we hosted interactive workshops where the youth could ask questions and talk about their experiences. We shared laughter, doubt, and pain. We discussed writing, archiving, Little Burgundy, art, creativity, issues within the Black community, poetry, and gardening, among other topics. The project became a genuine collaboration; through the power of networking, the community offered opportunity to our youth.

Linda Leith Publishing (LLP) took a particular interest in this work and enlisted our youth in the formation of *Font* magazine, when our creative pieces were published in the first issue in November, 2021. The next opportunity arose when we were introduced to Dave McKenzie, the founder and coordinator of the Concordia MBA Community Service Initiative. We welcomed the youth attending or interested in attending Concordia University, and Dave McKenzie led four mentorship sessions, getting to know us and offering his wisdom.

Our project participants were spotlighted at two book launch events: one for *The Fire That Time: Black Radicalism and the Sir George Williams Affair*, edited by Ronald Cummings and Nalina Mohabir, and one for the reissue of Mairuth Sarsfield's ground-breaking novel about Black Montreal, *No Crystal Stair* (LLP, 2021) and of its first-ever French translation, *En bas de la côte* (Linda Leith Éditions, 2022, trans. Rachel Martinez).

This project went well beyond authoring a book. The writers' willingness to engage with everyone who showed interest was gratifying. A community came together in support of the youth, gave them a voice, allowed them to situate themselves within the Black community, and helped them better understand themselves.

This project united youth from different neighbourhoods, backgrounds, and contexts. The connections forged led to beautiful collaborations, and the youth grew their personal networks in turn. We, as a team, established new community connections while strengthening existing relationships with other Black-led organizations. These bonds encourage solidarity in the community and work to sustain our history.

So, this project, initially created to produce only our book, evolved into something much greater. The youth we were lucky enough to work with grew as people and as artists. It was a privilege to peer into the minds of these capable, ambitious young people. As the project comes to an end, friendships are just beginning. To our writers: it has truly been a pleasure working with you all. We cannot wait to see what's next for you.

Spanning the period from the early 1890s to the present, these essays aim to capture the most important milestones in Montreal's Black history. *Where They Stood* will be a resource for all those willing to educate themselves on this largely untold history. Realizing how little written material there is documenting the contributions of Montreal's Black Anglos, we hope to have filled that gap to some degree and would like this book to serve as a resource in academic settings. More importantly, we hope to educate the intolerant, inform the ignorant, and appreciate the unseen, in our effort to create the change we wish to see in our society.

Introduction

For years, we have engaged in debates and power struggles about the creation of a widely inclusive democratic system in Canada and other countries of the world. The concept of democracy is essential to the social, cultural, economic, and political decision-making processes of any human society. It is key to the functioning of the economy, as well as the vitality and quality of life for all members of Canadian society.

However, some subgroups are "more equal" than others, and their human rights are more respected than those of others. Historically, white French- and English-speaking peoples have dominated Indigenous peoples, Blacks, and other people of colour in this land. The "Canada" we know today is a result of displacement of Indigenous peoples by European settlers who distributed the wealth of its ecosystems among themselves and their European societies.

The Europeans introduced a system of colonization and residential occupation backed by military power that supported a worldwide network of mercantilist production and trade. This involved the gathering and redistribution of mineral wealth, cultural artifacts, and human beings as slave labour to produce raw materials and goods for European consumption. Within this system, Canada became a colony of residence for settlers from multiple European countries (including France, Britain, Russia, Germany, Spain, etc.). During this period of colonization, the country was dominated by the British and the French. Their descendants remain the dominant classes.

To fully grasp the socio-economic and psychosocial status of Blacks and people of colour in today's Canada, one must understand how they came to represent 3-4 percent of the population today. How did they gain ground in a predominantly white-ruled country? How did they immigrate, settle, and make their space within the community?

Black migrants represented a very small number of people here prior to 1600, but the Black presence increased over time, especially after 1960. Canada participated in and benefited from the transatlantic slave trade that supplied labour to the colonies of the Americas and the Caribbean, especially to their sugar and cotton plantations. It was directly engaged in the buying and selling of slaves and the exploitation of free Black labour. The territory that would become Canada was an important component of the British position in the transatlantic slave trade. Canada directly benefited from supplying household consumer goods and domestic supplies, construction materials, and other goods to British colonies in the Caribbean in exchange for sugar, molasses, rum, bananas, cocoa, and citrus products.

Slavery was justified on the basis of French, British, and wider European claims of white racial superiority. This white supremacist doctrine was transported to the colonies to justify the ownership of humans, forced labour, and colonial occupation. Most infer that anti-Black sentiment in Canada was inspired by the practices of discrimination in the US, its engagement in the transatlantic slave trade, and, later, Jim Crowism. However, for those who have lived through the abuses of discrimination and anti-Black racism, Canadian racism and hatred seem deeply entrenched and personal. Canada's discrimination is systemic.

For hundreds of years the country sought to define itself in opposition to the United States, as a more humanitarian and welcoming society. It has, for example, described itself as the star of the North, a country of freedom and equality, the place where runaway slaves were received, and the endpoint of the Underground Railroad. Canadians often believe we do not subscribe to outdated, unpopular racist concepts. But Canada was born and bred in racist ideology. Despite claims of equal opportunity and access to justice, Canada's legal system has repeatedly curtailed the rights of minorities. For contemporary instances of this, one need only consider the "notwithstanding clause" in the constitution and recent Quebec legislation such as Bill 21, Bill 40, and Bill 96.[1]

White superiority has always prevailed in much of North America, whether outwardly or systemically. The thesis of racial superiority assigns a superior status to groups that control resources, thereby giving them disproportionate access to resources and success. At the same time, it downgrades and eliminates those that they consider inferior to their own racial subset. British historians, such as John Dalberg-Acton and Thomas

---

1   For references, sources, notes, links, and credits compiled by the Black Studies Research Centre and the authors for *Where They Stood*, please see: www.bcrc.wheretheystood.com.

Babington Macaulay, argued that certain races are a "negative" element in the world and that their existence depends on other, superior groups. Their "subjection," it follows, "to a people of higher capacity for government is of itself, no misfortune; it is the law of civil progress."

Canadian society saw intense debates surrounding multiculturalism as a state policy from the 1950s onwards. This was a broad response to the ranking of the subgroups in Canada, placing white English-speaking groups at the top, and non-whites and other minorities at the bottom.

Canadian sociologist John Porter described the emergent Canadian society and economy as a *Vertical Mosaic* in a 1976 book that captured the attention of Canada's social scientists, historians, and journalists. These two words captured the complex reality of Canada as a hierarchical patchwork of classes and ethnic groups. Class structures positioned Anglo-Saxon Protestants at the top, with everyone else lower down, and the term gained long-lasting social and political currency, underlining the notions of Canada as a nation of two solitudes and a "British fragment." In contrast with the American image of a melting pot, the concept of a vertical mosaic is includes strands of social and economic inequality, exclusion, and systemic discrimination, under a mask of mainstream linguistic protection and the historic duality of French and British rights and privileges.

Porter's critical analysis proved politically unsettling, arguing that Canadian society was "class-bound, marred by serious ethnic inequality, dominated by elites, and not democratic in any full sense of the term." Porter supplemented this description and analysis with a principled moral and logical critique of inequalities of class and power.

The 1960s saw the rise of revolutionary ferment in Quebec. Some groups, such as the Front de libération du Québec (FLQ), began to engage in violent confrontations and demand independence. In response, the Liberal Party of Canada, under Prime Minister Pierre Elliot Trudeau introduced a counterstrategy: the concept of *multiculturalism*, the Canadian movement away from biculturalism and bilingualism and towards overall cultural inclusivity. However, in Canada, with the emergence of Quebec nationalism and the francization of Quebec, we now have two vertical mosaics: one within Quebec, which is a province designated as a nation and in some ways treated as such, and one in English Canada. The white francophone Québécois has replaced the WASP at the top of the racial hierarchy in Quebec. French is the official language of Quebec, and the French-language laws Bill 96 and Bill 101 work together to make the Quebec vertical mosaic less dynamic, arguably less democratic, and in many cases discriminatory—the intention being to establish the historical French class at the top and English speakers at the bottom.

Outside of Quebec, English and French remain the two official languages. Special constitutional arrangements largely protect the rights and institutions of the two dominant groups of European settlers responsible for Canada's pre-twentieth-century ecosystem. The case can be made that the Official Languages Acts of 1969 and 1988 essentially divide the country into two spaces—French and English Canada—giving every provincial legislature the right to use what is known as the notwithstanding clause to impose measures that may abrogate human rights otherwise guaranteed by the Charter of Rights and Freedoms, with the intention of assimilation of all others into their dominant language and culture. In a study of communal identity formation, Professor of Social Work Buster Ogbuagu says it is "designed to develop and maintain Canada in a racial hierarchy as solely a white settler society." This argument was reinforced by Bill 101 and again by Bill 96.

Using the notwithstanding clause, Quebec has made French the province's official language and the legal language of business. It has restricted access to education in English and the provision of health and social services in English to English-speaking and Allophone residents and citizens of Quebec. Fundamentally, as Premier Legault stated recently, only persons born here and schooled in English in Quebec will have the right to receive education, health care, and government notices in English. He used Jamaican migrants as an example; those who come here from Jamaica will have to learn French and will *not* be entitled the protection of their linguistic rights under the constitution in Quebec.

Many Black scholars and organizations argue that de facto Blacks are considered a lower class in Quebec and that English-speaking Blacks in particular are not wanted here. They are not only discriminated against on the basis of colour and race but are reliving the experience of colonialism imposed by constitutional "arrangements" and government practices that act as a screen for anti-Black sentiments and systemic discrimination. It appears the constitutional changes from 1960 to 1990 were solely designed to protect those considered historically English and historically French in Quebec, who are majority white. All this to say, racism and discrimination in Canada are unrelenting, protected as they are by the will of the historic French majority and Bills 101 and 96.

This project attempts to capture the history of Blacks in Quebec, more specifically English-speaking Blacks, a group marginalized by their skin colour and a mother tongue inherited through the transatlantic slave trade and colonial capitalism. It primarily deals with the responses of Black leadership to changes in Quebec from the 1800s to now. We are concerned with gaps in knowledge and their effects on the ingenuity of Black communities. These gaps persist because of the continued refusal of Quebec society to address systemic discrimination.

We affirm the validity of Black resistance to these inequalities, showing how Black organization and engagement addresses the needs of the Black community, including some successes and failures in our persistent efforts to cross or eliminate the colour line.

Please see diagrams on pp. 182–184 demonstrating the relationships between Black organizations created between 1890 and 2006 in response to a number of changing social, economic, political, and environmental factors. The mapping shows the increase in the multiplicity of agents associated with social and political change, economic growth, as well as population expansion and diversification throughout Montreal and its surrounding regions.

Black populations prior to the 1960s were concentrated in the Saint Antoine neighbourhood, which became known as Little Burgundy, and are represented by clusters of agents in the northwest quadrant of the mapping. The agencies driving the social, cultural, and economic life of the community have been the Union United church, supported and sustained by the Coloured Women's Club, a social and economic force in the community of the time; the Negro Community Centre (NCC); and the Universal Negro Improvement Association (UNIA). The NCC is a core agency responsible for creating a bridge between the pre-sixties Canadian-born Black community and post-sixties Black immigrant populations. On the northeast quadrant are new populations creating new agencies and communities in other areas. These newer developments interact in a significant way with established Black agencies in the Little Burgundy community as they create a trans-generational and trans-cultural connectivity of Black resistance.

Black communities, notwithstanding differences in approaches and generations, came together to fight against the colour line in general, but specifically anti-Black racism and its manifestations in education, housing, employment, as well as social and cultural services. The unity of voices reflects how those of African ancestry have resisted the barriers set against them. Community leadership is often fragmented and based on country of origin. The perceived failure of this approach and its ability to eliminate systemic discrimination has led to the creation of the National Black Coalition, the Black Community Administration of Quebec, and its collaborations with the Little Burgundy Black community. These groups have worked together to create a network of outreach programs and alliances across Montreal and the surrounding regions (including the Black Community Associations of NDG, Côte-des-Neiges, LaSalle, the West Island, the South Shore, Verdun, etc.). This unification of leadership around common purposes fulfilled the need for specialization and standardization in terms of region and discipline.

Allowing communities to present a united front when dealing with mainstream French- and English-speaking leadership, was a pan-Black organizational network created by the NCC. This included the regional Black community associations plus several specialist agencies such as the Black Theatre Workshop (BTW), the Quebec Board of Black Educators (QBBE), the Black Community Forum (BCF), and by extension the Black Community Resource Centre (BCRC).

Relationships between community organizations and leadership voices were and remain neither smooth nor perfect. This is clear from the history of rivalries among the groups, which have included differing claims of being the first to provide key services of one kind or another, or internal and public debates about the effectiveness of radical as opposed to strategic approaches. Perfect examples are offered by scholars documenting the relative impacts of the radical Black power student movement in Montreal, the Montreal Congress of Black Writers in 1968, the National Black Coalition's claim to have been the first cross-country Black solidarity movement, as well as Carl Whittaker's pan-Black "communology" movement of the eighties and nineties. This is reflected in David Austin's book *Fear of a Black Nation*; the PhD thesis of P.C. Hebert,

"A Macrocosm of General Struggle: Black Thought and Activism in Montreal 1960–1969"; and Nalini Mohabir and Ronald Cummings' edited volume considering the clash of views around the Sir George Williams student protests entitled *The Fire That Time: Transnational Black Radicalism and the Sir George Williams Occupation.*

This struggle of the fragmented communities reflects the coexistence of different Black ethnicities, with immigrants from a variety of former colonies seeking to carve out spaces in primarily English- and French-speaking, white-dominated societies. This led to the creation of collaborative strategies in the face of the negative impact of extreme Quebec nationalism and systemic discrimination. The two bottom quadrants of the diagrams on pp. 182–184 partially represent where agencies in the Black communities as well as other ethnicities come together around certain issues like the abuse of rights and freedoms, social and health services, employability and employment, economic development problems, and the creation of policies that are more inclusive. Black Lives Matter is one manifestation of the coming together of many different ethnic and cultural groups to address the problem of racial hate, systemic discrimination, police brutality, and exclusion.

Chapter 1

We Stand Tall Wherever We Are: A Community that Defies Borders

Matthew Mullone

An in-depth understanding of our history is essential to evolving from our past. In pursuit of this mission, diving deep into the history of Black English-speaking culture in Montreal will allow for proper recognition of those who contributed to our community and its prosperity. To do that, we must first consider the Black communities that arrived in this corner of the continent, and how their struggles moulded the culture and character of this city.

First colonized by France in the 16th century, Quebec's culture continues to be influenced and informed by the French language to this day. It is the only jurisdiction in North America where French is the sole official and common language, both in law and daily life. In stark contrast to the rest of the province, Montreal has long thrived as a multilingual metropolis. Millions of immigrant families packed up the cultural treasures of their homelands and brought them as gifts to their new home. Among these families were those who composed Montreal's English-speaking Black community, which has had a lasting impact on a predominantly French-speaking space.

Black culture in Montreal is overlooked in Canadian history, likely due to Canada's white hegemonic landscape. While its existence is more widely acknowledged today, racial bias continues to pervade academic and literary circles. We need to acknowledge and remember the mass migration, settlement, and contributions to Montreal of all Black English speakers from the West Indies, the southern United States, and other Canadian provinces.

Black culture in North America was forged by a community of individuals who found themselves stripped of their identities in the wake of systemic subjugation, oppression, and discrimination during the early 20th century. Among the components of Black culture are the history of jazz and its movement from the southern United States to Montreal; the employment of Black men as railroad porters, which allowed for socio-economic progress in the Black community and encouraged further settlement and migration; and two community organizations whose emergence proved fundamental to the development of the Black English-speaking community in Quebec.

The Coloured Women's Club and the Union United Church, both of which emerged from the jazz age and the culture of widespread employment of Black men as railroad porters, ultimately transformed Saint Antoine—a bustling borough on the northern bank of the Lachine Canal—into the social and economic epicentre of English-speaking Black life in Montreal.

Jazz and Black Artistic Liberation

Jazz players used their music to form solidarity with one another in a world of white supremacy and racial inequity. In reaction to its rising popularity, white American rhetoric smeared jazz as deviant, reductive, and a threat to the hegemonic social order. Some even attempted to paint jazz as an inferior art by labelling it as a plagiarized imitation of classical European music. On the contrary, jazz attracted keen musical minds and ushered in the artistic whirlwind of the Black Renaissance.

To fully understand, respect, and love jazz, we must develop an appreciation of its musicians. Jazz was born slowly over many years on the streets of New Orleans, Louisiana. This riveting new genre of music had several influences including Creole slave songs, Negro Spirituals, Classical, Ragtime, and African rhythms. It counted amongst its earliest forerunners such talents as Edmund Dédé. A Creole New Orleans native born in 1827, Dédé was fortunate enough to be born free and train under the tutelage of Black composer Constantin Debergue and Italian violinist Ludovico Gabici. Perhaps even more impressive is that Dédé's own 1852 composition "Mon Pauvre Coeur" is the oldest known sheet music ever written by a person of colour.

Although Dédé was not a jazz musician, his example helped others in the Black community change their cultural landscape, paving the way for legendary figures like Charles Bolden. Dubbed the Father of Jazz, Charles "Buddy" Bolden was a trumpet player who captured the essence of New Orleans' musical spirit by incorporating the "brash, bluesy, raggy sound that created what we call jazz." While he never recorded any of his compositions himself, other jazz musicians keep his memory alive, telling his story by playing his tunes.

Community has always been at the heart of jazz. The music has served as a bridge, connecting neighbours and families for generations. A method of cultural exchange between peoples, jazz allowed for individuals to bond through the collaboration of music-making, without being limited by the barrier of the spoken word.

For the Black community, there was little opportunity to communicate and spread such cultural knowledge. Slavery and segregation had long restricted their access to education, resulting in higher rates of illiteracy and lower likelihood of socioeconomic advancement. These restrictions were a calculated tactic of the White majority to keep Black residents oppressed and subservient. However, jazz music offered a method of creative resistance. The genre unified otherwise isolated individuals and brought Black culture to the forefront of the music scene. It cultivated the spirit of African ancestors, creating a new and sophisticated conception of music that incorporated the ancestral rhythms from which the movement first took inspiration. As chronic victims of white colonialism, Black people managed to precisely adapt their musical styles to their exceptional communal experience, infusing their personalities into structures of classical European music. This experimentation allowed Black Americans to redefine their relationships to their African lineage once diminished by slavery. As the history of Black people was effectively erased by white supremacist and colonialist actors, jazz continued to bring ever-defiant attention to Black art and culture.

Jazz swept through the southern United States at a time when such an artistic revolution was needed in earnest. The abolition of slavery in 1865 and the Reconstruction period that followed resulted in the drafting of the notorious Jim Crow laws. Beginning in 1877, this heinous era embodied the lingering racism and hatred many white Americans harbored for their Black counterparts after the defeat of the Confederacy. Segregation policies in the southern states sabotaged Black families' efforts to improve their social and economic standing, solidifying racial and class divides between Black and white Americans in the South for another century.

The legislatures of these states designed such laws to deny Blacks their voting rights. Even worse, lynching became increasingly common. The horrific practice was often used as punishment and to promote fear, with local authorities sympathetic to, or in league with, the white supremacist perpetrators. The persistence of such cruel treatment forced southern Blacks to uproot themselves and travel north in search of opportunity and peace. It was through this mass exodus that Montreal became a meeting place for many Black migrants in search of refuge and equality.

Before this massive wave of migration across the Great Lakes and the Adirondacks, Black people had already been in Canada for over a hundred years. Many arrived by the transatlantic slave trade, making landfall around 1763, in tandem with the British conquest of New France. The colonial government of Quebec permitted and profited from slavery for generations, using sadistic punishment to instill fear in, and subjugate, the Black population.

One story in particular paints a vivid picture of the systemic devaluation and oppression of Black slaves, especially women. Marie-Joseph Angélique was an enslaved woman who was murdered by the government of Quebec after being accused of having set the Montreal fire of 1734. She became one of the first documented Black women in the country. Following her flawed conviction, Angélique suffered brutal torture; her legs were crushed, and she was ultimately hanged, her body displayed publicly for hours before being burnt. This demonstrates how white supremacy permeated Quebec society, highlighting the oppressive relationship between Blacks and the French colonial state.

Black communities began to grow in prominence throughout Ontario, Nova Scotia, and Manitoba. Though they were able to create a sense of home, life in Canada was by no means simple for Black American migrants. Yet their resilience in the face of adversity shows just how determined they were to survive amid harsh circumstances.

For Black American southerners coming in Montreal after tumultuous journeys, jazz offered comfort and a chance to retain their culture and family traditions while forging new community ties. A form of artistic protest for the Black community, the genre acted as a forum for self-expression and inclusion, often crossing the colour line and including white musicians. Jazz provided a place for peaceful communication between white and Black artists, as it did in its birthplace, New Orleans.

Porters and the Rise of the Black Working/Middle Class

In the nineteenth century, the Canadian railway accelerated the migration of West Indian and southern Black Americans to the city of Montreal. The completion of both the Grand Trunk and Canadian Pacific Railways in the late 1800s proved beneficial for the socioeconomic development of the city. The Canadian railway system was integral to the growth of the country and, in many ways, its induction into the modern age. The burgeoning train network connected communities, encouraged the building of cities, transported goods, and created jobs. Canada was on track to attain its goal of industrialized modernity and employed its developing railway technology to expand the economy.

For the Black community, the railway offered dreams of freedom and prosperity. However, government officials painted a picture of Black labourers, particularly porters, as peddlers of jazz and drugs, a threat to white morality. These images posed a potential threat to the Black community in Quebec.

A port and the nexus of many modes of travel in the late 1880s, Montreal became a major transportation hub and the headquarters for recruiting workers for the railways. When the Pullman Company introduced sleeping cars on their trains in 1867 to accommodate white passengers traveling long distances, it advertised Black men as servants, later known as sleeping car porters. Many Black people who arrived in Canada from the Caribbean were well educated but became porters due to limited job opportunities.

The Canadian government of the time believed its Black populace, though contributing to the country's economy, was not responsible enough for full citizenship. Originally, Black migration to Quebec was to be short-lived, the solution to a temporary labour shortage. A multitude of factors extended Black migrants' stay in Montreal, the most obvious being the attempt to escape the hardships of segregation and a lack of socioeconomic prospects in the American South. These individuals saw an opportunity to build and expand the Black community in Canada and begin anew.

In pursuit of this new life, many Black English speakers decided to set down roots in the working-class neighbourhood of Saint Antoine. Situated north of Montreal's Lachine Canal in the Southwest borough between Saint-Henri and Griffintown, Saint Antoine (later known as Little Burgundy) was instrumental in the growth, development, and prosperity of Montreal's Black English-speaking community. It was a meeting place for several Black migrant groups, a cultural hub defined by its openness to diversity.

A site of sharing between peoples with unique cultural experiences, Saint Antoine also provided Black residents with an array of economic opportunities. Canal-side factories were always in need of workers, and train stations began to attract Black men to work as porters. A camaraderie arose between these young men. The job, though perhaps a dignified advancement, by no means guaranteed a secure life. While work on the railway offered salary and solidarity, it also fortified and maintained pervasive racial biases against Black men, as the obedience to white patrons integral to the job reinforced their historic roles as servants.

The Pullman Company knew that Black workers from the southern states were far easier to exploit due to their former living conditions. These men came from poor, desperate, and vulnerable backgrounds; serving on trains was an improvement for themselves and their loved ones. They were obliged to work long hours—sometimes over a hundred hours a week—facing sleep deprivation and earning subpar wages on which they could barely keep their families afloat.

As porters, Black men were expected to meet every need of their white passengers. The railway companies knew that Black men were less likely to resist the barbarous conditions of the porter's life or unionize, unlike many white men in the same socioeconomic class. Tips from passengers also became an additional yet necessary supplement to their minimal wage. The porters relied on the steady flow of tips, and this also served as a psychological tactic to keep Black men subservient. The tipping system reinforced the very nature of service, keeping porters trapped in a dynamic of dependency while reinforcing the hierarchy between Black servers and their white customers.

Such subordination ensured Black people knew their place amongst the whites. This was one of the many ways in which white supremacy continued to colour the social fabric of North America. Despite their plight, Black men and women persisted and refused to be seen as anything less than equal.

Struggles for Black Migrants

Jim Crow proved extremely difficult to escape for many Black migrant families, as Canada had started to take cues from its neighbour to the south. White Canadians smeared Blacks as a threat to the modernization of their communities, fundamentally altering the identity of their nation.

William D. Scott, Superintendent of Immigration, was the gatekeeper for the Canadian border during the early 20th century. He believed that the solution to the country's sudden "Black problem" was to send Black people back to Africa, thereby maintaining Canada under the dominion of an Anglo-Saxon majority. Roughly 5,000 Black people from both the West Indies and the southern United States arrived in Canada looking for security, citizenship, and equality between 1870 and 1914, which were low levels in comparison to the numbers of immigrants from other countries at the time. Discrimination against Black people proved pervasive and incredibly cruel despite their hopes of a better life up north. Neither their fluency in English nor their shared Christianity offered them acceptance in white society.

In the half-century that followed Confederation, the young country strived to prove itself as a sovereign settler-colonial power, and racial equality was antithetical to such a state. The government's focus was on keeping the Dominion of Canada as white as possible by excluding Indigenous persons and people of colour from equal participation in public life and politics. Immigration policies increasingly reflected the racist trepidation of white Canadian citizens. These fears were most often directed at southern Black Americans, eventually manifesting as federal segregation laws to deter further migration. The administration of Prime Minister Wilfrid Laurier, for instance, went so far as to spread propaganda that Canadian winters were too harsh for Black migrants to survive.

Ever nervous about what white Canadians perceived to be the increasing "Africanization" of their society, the Laurier government passed the Canadian Immigration Acts of 1906 and 1910, which legislated discrimination against Black people on the basis of race. Both the United States and Canadian governments saw Black migration as a demographic problem and did not want it to compromise their relationship. The Canadian government often discouraged Black Americans from migrating to Canada and sent them instead to Central America. The United States government even wrote in a letter saying they would not be offended if the Canadian government denied Black Americans access to Canada. The Canadian government legally excluded Black Americans from migrating to Canada between 1906 and 1910, believing they were "undesirable," sometimes going so far as hiring Black Canadians to lobby against Black American immigration. This is most likely because Black Americans strongly resisted white supremacy in the South and were ready for combat when it came to defending their rights. Black Americans were considered violent and disobedient because they did not accept their dehumanization.

In 1912, the newly elected government of Prime Minister Robert Borden thought it could entice and manipulate Black West Indians into migrating to Canada in lieu of Blacks from the American South, believing the former to be better suited to railway work given their long subordination to British colonial rule. According to the Canadian government of the day, West Indians would better serve the Canadian railways because the British had for generations indoctrinated Black people to use their bodies to service the white ruling class. Both the Canadian and Quebec governments planned, indirectly or directly, to maintain their power over Black minds and bodies to preserve white hegemony.

At the turn of the 20th century, Black people faced mounting institutional prejudice from both Canada and the United States. They had no in the cultural imaginary of either country, whose laws and policies insinuated that Black people were incapable of civility, and should not be included in any decision-making processes. As Sarah-Jane Mathieu put it, "White Supremacy [was] used as a rational model of modernity and civility."

The Pullman Company used this idea to their advantage, hiring Black men solely as porters, which kept them at the bottom of the hierarchy. These were extremely violent times between white and Black people. The government capitalized on white citizens' racial anxiety and the desperation of Black people to keep the latter subordinate. White citizens of both countries could be relentless in rejecting Blackness, whether by threats of lynching or humiliating segregation.

Montreal had a large population of West Indians who had a strong foothold in North American politics, having long demanded they be afforded the same treatment and respect as other subjects of the British Empire. Slavery in the West Indies ended between 1834 and 1838, 30 years before its abolition in the United States, but colonialist structures still prevailed.

In contrast to their Caribbean counterparts, Black southerners were well versed in dealing with violent white supremacy, allowing them to better navigate the ongoing racist practices in Canada. These two Black populations were united by this knowledge and used it to form a stronger community. Ultimately, the porter job was empowering and profitable for many Black men. Jazz and the men who worked as porters paved the way for future generations of Black English speakers in Montreal.

The Achievements of Black Women for Montreal

Alongside jazzists and porters, Black women made profound contributions to their community. They provided community services, engaged in advocacy, expanded employment, and helped with the education of youth. The Coloured Women's Club (CWC) was started by porters' wives in Saint Antoine who, in 1902, began to contest what they declared to be the "persistent structural inequity and racialized colonial hierarchy."

While Canada continued to attempt to exclude the Black community from Canadian public discourse, the CWC began networking, fighting to restructure the hierarchy, and challenge racism. The CWC also promoted Black feminism, using their experience as Black women to critique racism and gender oppression, adding further analysis of how power and privilege are manifested and used to subdue minority groups within other minority groups.

These women came from varied backgrounds, representing many socioeconomic circumstances, cultural traditions, and political views. They changed the trajectory of the community by providing resources that catered to its specific needs. They combatted segregation by organizing against the narrative of anti-Blackness. Matilda Mays and Anne Greenu—the latter being the first president of the CWC—were able to open shelters and create soup kitchens during epidemics between 1904 and 1905. In a matter of years, the CWC evolved from a social club to an aid organization. It challenged the racist notions of their society through its members' collective and humanitarian actions, laying the foundation for Black solidarity in the fight for equality between the races and the sexes, and altered the public's perception of Black women in the process. The CWC offered something new to the community of Black English speakers in Quebec. They created a space in which everyone, from diverse backgrounds, could assemble with a sense of unity that was previously inconceivable. The CWC promoted a transnational pride that continued to develop among individuals of Montreal's African diaspora.

In Quebec houses of worship, a de facto colour bar was enforced, as was the case in many other parts of Canada. Black worshippers were placed in the back pews, limiting their movement and participation. Within a religion that touts its values of love, acceptance, and inclusion, the Black community found itself inhibited in its spiritual practice by the racism of these institutions. The CWC considered this an opportunity for communal solidarity and used this segregation as motivation to establish the oldest Black church in Canada. Founded in 1907, the Union United Church promoted unity amongst Black youth and encouraged them to take leadership roles for the future of Black Montreal. The church's programs were a direct call to action, providing an image of the Black community that was centred around self-worth and value. This was hard to reinforce in a society where Black individuals are treated as second-rate citizens. Preachers were revered as role models for younger congregants, while wearing their melanin with pride.

It is even more extraordinary that the church built their community outreach on the efforts of the CWC. Of the church's first twenty-six leaders, many were women who supported the community while men worked on the trains. The social mobility Black men attained as porters despite white oppression was made possible through the support, leadership, and strength of Black women. In consequence, Montreal's English-speaking Black community became a force for collective good, not to be underestimated or undervalued.

Conclusion

To this day, there is a continuing struggle for true equality among all peoples that make up Canadian society. Canadian governments have manipulated the image of the Black community for centuries to exercise racial control. The Quebec government also discriminates against the Black community based on their prejudiced views of who ought to call Quebec home.

The Black community has been and continues to be a leader in the fight for racial and social justice. Jazz culture helped break down the colour barrier constructed to divide and control the community. The Coloured Women's Club and the Union United Church also helped to unite Black English-speaking Montrealers, offering its members a net of safety and support. Black women engaged in community-building and Black cultural promotion by investing in religion and music, which could be shared by all. Though we still live in a world where individuals struggle to feel accepted, the foundation for a better life and a brighter future was laid in the small streets of Saint Antoine.

Chapter 2

"One God! One Aim! One Destiny!" Wartime Activism and Early Postwar Garveyism, 1914–1919

Sherwins Jean

On Tuesday, November 19, 1918, Montreal's streets bustled with a frenzy of postwar excitement. A week after the Allied Powers signed the armistice, ending the Great War, an African-American couple—chemist Norris Augustus Dodson and Lilian A. Dodson (née Berry)—went with four of their friends to Loew's Theatre in Montreal. As the city's "grandest movie palace," Loew's was located on the corners of Mansfield and Sainte-Catherine until it shut its doors in October 1999. The Dodsons, whose skin was light enough to pass as white, enjoyed an entertaining evening, but their unmistakably Black friends did not share the same experience. After being instructed by an employee to wait at the side, they were formally denied admission to the facility. A commotion and legal battles ensued.

In 1919, Dodson took their case to the Court of King's Bench, the province's court of appeal. According to court records, as detailed in historian Eric Reiter's book, *Wounded Feelings: Litigating Emotions in Quebec, 1870–1950*, the African-American man's defence relied on the argument of breach of contract. The purchase of the six cinema tickets acquired ahead of time constituted a legally binding agreement between the group and the venue. By denying entry to some of Dodson's friends, the venue was executing only part of that contract and thus violated it. Although the theatre's legal team denied any accusations of racial discrimination, it was clear that this had been an attempt at curating yet another white-only space.

It was not uncommon to be refused service because of one's Blackness. Justice Fortin concluded that Dodson's belligerent attitude and disorderly conduct accounted for the theatre's refusal of entry and the bench sided with Loew's Theatre's, thereby setting a precedent allowing the discriminatory practice of denying Black patrons access to theatre venues or restricting them to balcony seats. In 1921, two years after Dodson v. Loew's Theatre, the cinema began publicizing the upper balcony seats, reserved for Black patrons, as "monkey cages." The ruling had granted private business owners the power of discretion and contributed to Canada's racism problem.

Segregation in Canada was—and one could argue still is—a matter of implicit, poorly hidden racism that the system, as evidenced in Dodson v. Loew's Theatre, boldly reinforced. This is ostensibly unlike the United States, where discrimination has been historically codified through the Jim Crow laws. Canadians pride themselves on their purported absence of a colour line. In the context in which Frederick Douglass coined the term "colour line," this "broad enough and black enough" line served as a metaphor for the social, political, and economic separation of Blacks and whites after the abolition of slavery. It divides society in a way that favours white supremacy and denigrates racialized others.

The false supposition of Canada being a colour-blind utopia appeared around the same time African Americans trekked north via the Underground Railroad. As they sought freedom from slavery and persecution in the United States, African Americans saw Canada as the Promised Land. This myth, Canadian historian James W. St. G. Walker argued, was the major feature differentiating Canadians from Americans. What truly distinguished Canada from its southern neighbour was its ability to deny its racism. Although the British Slavery Abolition Act of 1834 protected African American migrants from re-enslavement, Canada was not as idyllic as was advertised. Beginning in the early 20th century, the increasing northward migration of African Americans to Canada amplified this false narrative.

The "pacifying insufficiency of Blacks," according to Dalhousie University scholar Lloyd W. Brown, explains this assumption of better treatment: the low number of Black people in the country meant that the Black population was not a preoccupation for the white majority.

As more Blacks emigrated, however, anti-Blackness became a prevalent phenomenon nationwide, particularly in the context of the country's nation-building project. In telling the story of the No. 2 Construction Battalion, Canada's first all-Black, segregated military unit, this chapter aims to shed light on Canada's racism in the context of the Great War and how it catalyzed the organization of pro-Black Canadian movements in the early 20th century. Marcus Garvey's Universal Negro Improvement Association (UNIA), for example, was, in the words of Trinidadian-Canadian author Dionne Brand, "the first secular movement to rival the magnetism of the churches" in Black Canadian communities.

Canada in World War I, 1914–18

As a dominion of the British Empire, Canada's involvement in World War I began when Great Britain declared war against Germany in August 1914. Called the Great War, the conflict owes its moniker to the horrifying scale and immense cost in human lives. Unprecedentedly, the war mobilized millions of people worldwide, involved imperial powers and their colonies, and was fought on numerous geographical fronts.

For Canada, the war presented an opportunity to support the motherland. It was also a chance for the burgeoning country to forge its own national identity. Arguably, it did so by enacting policies of internal economic development, strengthening national values, and reinforcing white supremacist ideals.

As early as the 1880s, the Canadian government attempted to curtail Asian immigration by establishing anti-Asian laws. The 1885 Chinese Immigration Act, for example, imposed a hefty head tax of fifty dollars per Chinese newcomer, rendering their immigration more costly and difficult. Frustrated with these racist laws, protesters demonstrated against anti-Asian social and political exclusion policies in the 1907 Vancouver Race Riots. In response to these protests, Canadian statesman William Lyon Mackenzie King argued that, "Canada should remain a white man's country," since it "is to be not only desirable for economic and social reasons… [it] is necessary on political and national grounds."

This statement reflects the racist attitudes of many Canadian officials at the time, in Parliament and military ranks. King would be elected prime minister of Canada in 1921.

As the war raged on, both material and human resources quickly depleted. By 1916, desertion, massive casualties, and a decline in volunteer participation sapped the Canadian army's military strength. Not a single battalion formed once the army reached its maximum capacity. In response, Prime Minister Sir Robert Laird Borden and other government officials deliberated on the possibility of a mandatory military draft. Eventually, Parliament enforced conscription through the Military Service Act in 1917. Concurrently, Indigenous, Asian, and Black Canadians were denied the right to enlist nationwide. Despite facing rejection, scores of Black Canadians, motivated by their sense of patriotism, attempted to volunteer in the war effort. Many saw themselves as loyal British subjects first and foremost. Others believed directly contributing to the war effort would facilitate their inclusion in society. When they presented themselves to recruiting stations, however, most Black soldiers were turned away.

These occurrences were widespread across the country. In response, on November 6th, 1914, Arthur Alexander, a Black Ontarian from North Buxton, dedicated a letter to the federal minister of Militia and Defence Sir Sam Hughes. In this correspondence, Alexander inquired why healthy Black men were being refused the right to enlist if they were legally entitled to do so. Arthur concluded that it was for no apparent reason other than the colour of their skin, to which Sir Hughes responded that this matter was out of his power.

Hughes claimed it was not about race but based on the principle that the country's military was decentralized, meaning commanding officers had the right to accept or refuse whomever requested to join their ranks.

This form of racial gaslighting—the phenomenon of making racialized communities doubt their perceptions of racism—recurs throughout Canadian history. As evidenced in Dodson v. Loew's Theatre, Canadian officials continued to feign racial colour-blindness. They blamed Dodson's hostility when asked to exit the cinema instead of acknowledging the flagrant racism to which he had been subjected. Similarly, to the issue Alexander raised, the Acting Adjutant General W. E. Hodgins stated the "final approval of any man, regardless of colour or other distinction" rested in the hands of the units' commanding officers. The responses of Sam Hughes and other officials did not reflect their real attitudes toward Black soldiers. Reports show most officials believed the conflict was a "white man's war" and that Blacks were considered unfit to join the military for stereotypical reasons such as laziness, brutishness, and other supposed biological predispositions.

Black Canadians persisted, however, by continuing to present themselves to different stations across the nation. From British Columbia to Nova Scotia, they hoped to be accepted into the army. For example, according to military records, Maltese-born Corporal Daniel Hugh Livingstone succeeded in joining the ranks of the 158th Battalion in Vancouver, British Columbia. As more instances of racism came to light, notably via newspaper, the formation of the No. 2 Battalion was approved by Ottawa on July 5, 1916, granting Black Canadians the right to join the militia.

The No. 2 Construction Battalion

The digitized military records of the No. 2 Construction Battalion soldiers are now available for public consultation through Canada's Library and Archives website. Amongst those records can be found particulars concerning the soldiers' place of birth, family members, physical characteristics, and information about their unit transfers. The Black soldiers who succeeded in joining the Canadian Expeditionary Forces before the creation of this battalion, like Corporal Livingstone, were transferred to the all-Black unit.

Jamaican-born Canadian Private Robert A. Wildman, of the 167th Battalion in Quebec City, was also transferred to the segregated battalion. As reported by his military records, he had a "clear complexion" and "blue eyes." This physical description hints Wildman could have been a white-passing Black man. The colour of his skin, however, did not make him any less Black, and he hence joined the ranks of the No. 2 Construction Battalion in 1917. Those same military records, analyzed by Gordon Douglas Pollock in *Black Soldiers in a White Man's War*, also exposed more of the racism these soldiers experienced during the war. According to his findings, the Canadian Expeditionary Force (CEF) over-policed the soldiers of the No. 2 Construction Battalion. Pollock argues they were also overdisciplined. In this unit, a third of the members were, at one point or another, judged guilty of offenses "serious enough" to earn considerable punishments like being tied to a wagon wheel for hours or days at a time. Their situation is comparable with that of the 22nd Infantry Regiment, Quebec's French-speaking military corps, which the CEF created to segregate them from the English-speaking Canadian armed forces. Both units' soldiers were discriminated against due to their minority status: one on the basis of language and the other, race.

Out of its authorized manpower of 1,049 volunteers, the battalion recruited 670 men, 346 of whom were Canadian born. Out of the eleven volunteers that enlisted in Montreal, two resided in the city: Private William Isaac Taylor and Private Robert A. Wildman. The nine other soldiers had come from the British West Indies, Nigeria, the United States, and other Canadian provinces. This data is significant because it represents the demographics existing within Montreal's Black community: its members came from various parts of the Black world. Recruitment for the battalion was done through different channels, namely through churches and African-Canadian newspapers like the *Canadian Observer* and the *Atlantic Advocate*. However, the recruitment frenzy did not last long. According to historian Calvin Ruck, low participation can be explained by "previous rejection and humiliation of black volunteers; Blacks objecting to serving in a segregated non-combatant labour battalion; and the blatant exclusion of potential Black immigrants, particularly in Western Canada." As the result of inadequate recruitment techniques, desertions, and failing health, only 605 soldiers made it onto the S.S. Southland in Halifax, on March 25th, 1917. After less than two weeks, on April 7th, the men arrived in the English coastal city of Liverpool. Later, they were transferred to work in a Canadian mill in La Joux, France, in the Jura Mountains.

Upon their arrival on foreign soil, the troops were immediately tasked with non-combatant duties. The experiences of Black soldiers were much like those they had back home: they were met with "rejection, limitation, and [forced into] consignment to fill the supportive position[s]." Due to the lack of manpower and racist constraints, such as the belief that "killing Germans was the privilege of white troops," the No. 2 Construction Battalion did not fight the enemy on the frontlines. Instead, they supported another unit, the No. 5 Canadian Forestry Corps, by cutting and hauling logs, which later served in the construction of trenches. They made railroad ties with the Canadian Railway Troops and ensured the Allied soldiers always had enough water. Although seemingly insignificant, some historians have highlighted the battalion's role as essential in the Allied victory. Through their tasks, they sustained the smooth operation of daily endeavors. The Black soldiers' work proved vital to their white peers in the Western theatre. It was not until July 2022, however, that the federal government formally apologized to the soldiers and their families for how they were treated. This recognition came 104 years after the end of the war.

The experience of the No. 2 Construction Battalion pushed Black soldiers to fight for their rights as citizens of Canada and the British Empire. Historian Melissa N. Shaw argues the situation prompted a new wave of race consciousness in Ontario and across Black communities nationwide. To publicize the initial rejection these men faced after the outbreak of war in December 1914, the *Canadian Observer*, a Black Canadian newspaper based in Ontario, was launched. It was in publication until

1919. Dubbed by Shaw as the community's "war-baby," this newspaper adopted tones like those of American race papers circulating at the time. The journal was specifically created in response to Black men being barred from joining the Canadian Expeditionary Forces. This coincided with the influence on Black nationalists and activists of Marcus Garvey's Pan-Africanist ideologies. In Montreal, his influence culminated in the creation of a division of the Universal Negro Improvement Association in 1919.

Marcus Garvey and the Universal Negro Improvement Association

Marcus Mosiah Garvey Sr. bore many titles: political activist, publisher, entrepreneur, and heroic figure to many. Born in Saint Ann's Bay, Jamaica in 1887, Garvey was a descendant of Jamaican maroons—former slaves who either ran away or acquired their liberty from their masters. As a young man, he excelled in academics, and education later became a founding tenet of Garveyism. According to a 1963 biography written by Amy Jacques—Garvey's second wife—his father described him as having an "insatiable thirst for knowledge." In 1909, at the age of twenty-one, he briefly moved to Costa Rica to work as a timekeeper at the United Fruit Company, where his uncle had been a labourer. Garvey also worked on the construction of the Panama Canal.

During that trip, Garvey witnessed first-hand the horrifying treatment his Black peers endured outside of Jamaica. He noticed as he travelled through Latin America, in countries like Colombia and Venezuela, that anti-Black sentiment was present there as well. Blacks all over Latin America were treated poorly. He proceeded to ask the British consul about his observations. Since Black people of his home land of Jamaica held British West Indian status, Garvey posited that they were entitled to the same protections as any other subject of the British Empire. He further inquired about the consul's plan to better the conditions of the Black British subjects he had repeatedly seen mistreated. He received a tepid response to his demands. Indeed, the reactions of the British consul exemplified a sheer disregard for Black lives and an assumption that all Black people should be treated as second-class subjects. Canadian officials would show a similar disregard for Black men trying to enlist during the Great War. It was then that Garvey realized that if Black people did not care for themselves, then no one would.

Upon his return to Jamaica in 1911, Garvey sought to uplift all Blacks worldwide for the betterment of the Negro race. To privilege their political relations with Latin American governments, the Jamaican government showed initial "disinterestedness" in addressing and challenging the discrimination Black people faced in those countries. This reluctance to engage in pro-Black activism motivated Garvey to establish the Universal Negro Improvement Association (UNIA) in 1914, in the country's capital of Kingston. With its motto, "One God, One Aim, One Destiny," the association aimed to unite Blacks from all over the world in fulfilling God's will to emancipate them from mental slavery, "because whilst others might free the body, none but ourselves [Black people] can free the mind."

Three years later, on June 12th, 1917, the organization's first North American division opened in Harlem,

New York, the polestar of Black culture at the time. Unfortunately, the Harlem chapter closed its doors not long after, in 1927, due to poor management. Despite this setback, with Pan-Africanism at the core of this movement's philosophies, the organization carried on elsewhere with great success, notably in Canada.

The UNIA in Montreal

Montreal plays an important part in the history of the UNIA in Canada. After attending one of Garvey's conferences in Harlem, Egerton Langdon, a Montreal resident of Grenadian origin, invited the influential orator to give a speech north of the American border. In the winter of 1917, Garvey arrived in Canada, making Montreal the first of many stops in his quest to grow the UNIA in North America.

A year later, at one of Garvey's conferences in the city, Langdon's niece Louise met an African-American man named Earl Little. The two later got married and went on to have many children, one of whom grew up to be Malcolm Little, later known as Malcolm X.

On June 9th, 1919, the city's division of the UNIA opened its doors to the public. Initially headquartered at 243 Saint Antoine Street, the chapter was first located in the same building as the Canadian Pacific Railway's living quarters, where Montreal's Black porters took temporary housing. Even before the UNIA took root there, the establishment was already a "veritable drop-in centre and meeting place for Blacks" in Montreal. It was one of the few places in the city where they could meet freely without fear of being discriminated against or harassed.

The initiation fees for the members were $0.60, with annual dues of $4.20, of which $3.00 were kept for the local organization. These fees were used to fund programs like plays, extracurricular activities for children, and free hall rentals for events. The New York headquarters benefited from the remaining $1.20, and the money contributed to a communal funerary fund. One could either hold an active or ordinary membership. The former referred to those who financially contributed to the organization; ordinary, or passive, members referred to "all persons of Negro blood and African ancestry," meaning the association considered all Blacks to be members. Upon an active member's death, the family would be given $75 to help cover funeral expenses.

According to Leo W. Bertley's thesis, by 1925 fifteen divisions of the organization had opened in Canada. Although mostly located in the country's major cities, others developed in regions with less prominent Black communities. Some of these locations included Truro, Nova Scotia; Winnipeg, Manitoba; and Vancouver, British Columbia. The Black population on the Prairies and the West Coast was not as substantial as that in Ontario and Nova Scotia. However, many of the recent immigrants that settled in those regions had been part of the then-ongoing Great Northward Migration. In 1928, according to Wilfred Israel, the Black community of Montreal was 50 percent American, 40 percent West Indian, and 10 percent Canadian. Highly critical of the lack of race consciousness the native-born Canadians had developed by then, Israel described them as "rural and small-town dwellers," who had adopted the "practices of the whites." Americans had brought over race papers and West Indians encountered other Blacks through their migration. Consequently, they, much like Garvey in Panama, had witnessed the racism and discrimination against their peers. African Canadians were dispersed across a large and sparsely settled landscape, making it difficult for them to form strong, close-knit communities.

In its heyday around 1922, Montreal's division of the UNIA counted approximately seven hundred active members. Henry Hall, the division's first president, can be credited for those numbers, having recruited approximately four hundred in the organization's first year alone. As the UNIA was notorious for poor bookkeeping, however, the numbers are not accurate. Former Montreal Garveyites have recalled that there were far more members than what records indicate.

By 1928, only about two hundred members remained. Israel explained this dwindling in membership by pointing to the issue of emigration: by the early to mid-1920s, many of the community members moved to the United States. The current UNIA treasurer, Mervyn Weekes, who was interviewed for this chapter, also posited that as more West Indians migrated to Montreal, culture-specific organizations took over, surpassing the Pan-Africanist association's influence in the city's Black community. The Vincentians, Trinidadians, Barbadians, and Jamaicans, to name a few, formed their own associations to rally people together. These groups provided an opportunity for migrants to keep their cultures alive. They addressed domestic and political issues, and offered specific cultural celebrations and traditions, like carnivals, which the UNIA could not accomplish.

In 1943, the Montreal UNIA completed their biggest achievement and purchased a building on the corners of Saint Jacques and Fulford streets (now Georges-Vanier). Unfortunately, as part of the green line Metro extension, the city demolished the building on March 18th, 1984, and replaced it with condos. Before its demolition, the building had fourteen low-rent housing units, commercial spaces, and a restaurant. Although they received little compensation for the expropriation of the building—"three times nothing," according to Henry J. Langdon, then president of the UNIA—they still managed to acquire another building in 1994. Now located at 2741 Notre-Dame Street West, the UNIA is still in the heart of the Saint Antoine (now Little Burgundy) district, "between the tracks and below the hill." Its success, historians have suggested, comes from effective leadership, notably that of Mr. Langdon. According to Weekes, successfully following Garvey's main teachings also aided the chapter.

Garveyism aims for the liberation and celebration of Black people all over the world. To achieve this goal, Garvey believed members of the African diaspora and continental Africans should be supportive of themselves and not rely solely on external sources. "Whatever happens, happens because we make it happen," Weekes wrote. Mutual aid amongst people of African descent was essential to the success of Blacks globally. To this day, the Montreal chapter of the UNIA does not take any grants or subsidies from the government and rather chooses to operate independently, just as Garvey intended.

As of 2022, the Montreal branch of the UNIA is still active and keeps in touch with the Toronto and

Nova Scotian divisions, although involvement with the organization has dwindled since the onset of the COVID-19 pandemic. They still offer scholarships and some of the activities the Island organizations could not, like more flexible schedules in terms of rental space. Funeral funds, hall rentals, and after-school programs for children in Little Burgundy still exist. They also host a myriad of cultural programs, notably during Black History Month, like the 2016 Jazz in the Neighbourhood event which celebrated some of Montreal's Black jazz artists. All proceeds went to the UNIA's Scholarship Fund.

In 2019, to celebrate the hundredth anniversary of the opening of the Montreal chapter, the Montreal division received a plaque commemorating it as an Event of National Historic Significance from the government of Canada. Currently the commemorative sign, designed by Parks Canada, proudly rests on the front of the building. The UNIA also works with other organizations to help mutually uplift and attract more people. The Union United Church and the UNIA, for example, have joined hands in the Kwanzaa program. They seek to continue teaching that Black people should be independent, but not hyper-independent. For the past fifteen years, the UNIA has also owned fourteen subsidized apartment units, where residents only pay 25 percent of their income to cover rent, heating, electricity, and building maintenance. The remaining 75 percent is covered by the city of Montreal. As long as the building was occupied by Black people, the two parties agreed, it could not be sold, as it had been in 1982. The building, Weekes said in the interview, will always be co-owned by the UNIA and the city. In the event of a vacancy, the city is not allowed to rent it out. Rather, the UNIA oversees the selection process. For example, if a white couple and a Black couple are both interested in a unit, the latter will be prioritized. In effect, the main tenets of Garveyism are kept alive.

Conclusion

While the many battles fought by Black Canadians against racism can be traced back to events and protests prior to the 20th century, it is in the early 1900s and the subsequent decade that we begin to witness a boom in Black activism and affirmation. Through their resistance, the No. 2 Construction Battalion soldiers paved the way to unite Afro-Canadians, native-born or otherwise, in combating racism in the country. Their will and determination to be recognized as citizens with all associated rights mirrored Marcus Garvey's philosophy as they continued to spread amongst Montreal's Black community. His teachings and the overall increased awareness of Black issues in the community eventually led to a surge in the establishment of Black spaces in a white-dominated city. Saint Antoine was not only a hub for Blacks, but also rapidly became an entertainment centre known worldwide. Jazz artists and "fanatics" alike flocked to the cabarets and clubs in the borough, such as Rockhead's Paradise, giving Montreal its then nickname of Sin City. Many Americans, like Norris Augustus Dodson, came to the party city to enjoy themselves, and escape the American moral crusades of the early 1900s.

Chapter 3

A Place Called Home

Anne Victoria Jean-François

During the Prohibition era, organized crime from the United States funneled its way into Montreal, reshaping the city. While Prohibition was law in the United States and many parts of Canada, Montreal was an exception. Alcohol was readily available in what was called "The Paris of the North." In the 1920s, Montreal became more vibrant, with many dance halls, vaudeville theatres, bars, and nightclubs. The demand for workers grew. Jobs as sleeping car porters, cooks, waiters, and domestic workers opened up for the Black working class. In the Saint Antoine area, isolated boarding houses sheltered temporary and permanent residents. This housed the Black workforce that was required to be in near proximity to its places of employment. Black-run businesses started to concentrate in that area to accommodate the needs of a growing community, like Rockhead's Paradise, a night club which lit up the streets of Montreal in 1928.

Saint Antoine's perseverance through the problematic social climate of the 1920s in part stems from the influence of Caribbean revolutions and the ideologies therein, those that encouraged Black people to demand more than the crumbs provided to them. It is said that the 1920s was the golden period of Montreal's Black history, bringing millions of immigrants to the city. However, very little is said about the oppression experienced in the servitude to which Black folks were relegated in the labour market.

The success of Rufus Rockhead—owner of Rockhead's Paradise—embodies this Caribbean revolution and evolution. It is essential to understand the different impacts colonial systems have had on the spirit and self-worth of Black Montrealers, and how these affected the growth of a people. This includes not only the movements of Caribbean history but the spirit of African Americans and other freedom seekers.

Black Employment and Social Services

Rufus Rockhead returned to Montreal following World War I on March 19th, 1919. When he arrived in Montreal, he was limited to being a sleeping car porter. The consistent income of sleeping car porters sustained many Black community members who occupied the east coast railroad cities, such as Montreal and its Windsor Station. Of Black men in Montreal, 90 percent were sleeping car porters, servicing white passengers who travelled to and from Montreal. The word spread that there were "great" work opportunities for Black men as sleeping car porters in Montreal, and a significant influx of Black people arrived in the city throughout the 1920s. With them came a variety of food, culture, and art; jazz artists from all parts of the USA came to Montreal. These musicians and porters played an essential role in creating Montreal's reputation as a cultural epicentre.

At this point, the predominantly Black community of Saint Antoine lacked social support structures. The crime and dissolute habits associated with the lively

Montreal nightlife had ill effects on vulnerable families. The government would only begin to provide social assistance in the early 1920s. The University of Toronto established a social work training program in 1914, followed by McGill University in 1918, and the Canadian Association of Social Workers was later founded in 1926.

Quebec's economy grew strongly during this period, and its population expanded from 1.5 million to 2.9 million. Montreal accounted for 35 percent of the province's population by the 1930s. Numerous railroads, large banks, and other corporations helped Montreal become an important economic driver for Western Canada, as prairie wheat was exported to Europe from its port. Montreal remained Canada's leading industrial centre and made up two-thirds of the value of Quebec manufacturing.

Most French Canadians were forced to work in farming and factories. Economic power was concentrated in the hands of a few Montreal capitalists early in the century, who were nearly all English Canadians. This kept the French-Canadian bourgeoisie to a marginal position in limited local institutions and traditional sectors.

In the 1920s, in the United States and parts of Canada, the production, distribution, and sale of alcohol were prohibited. This prompted a surge in bootlegging, some of which by organized crime. Infamous mobsters from New York and Chicago like Lucky Luciano and Al Capone were lured to Montreal, which was an exception among mostly dry Quebec municipalities, with its free-flowing booze. These mobsters exploited the city's red-light district and its port. Cops also played a part by turning a blind eye to organized crime for a cut of the profits, making Montreal a playground for lawbreakers. This took place in a context of poverty and labour exploitation.

In response, social services and unionization slowly gained momentum. Unions and other organizations provided workers with a voice in politics, calling for electoral reform, free and compulsory education, social programs, and the nationalization of public utilities during the period 1886–1930. These demands were part of the labour movement's "*projet de société*," emphasizing reform rather than the abolition of capitalism.

In the early 1920s, the government began to provide social supports. The growth of unions led to better working conditions. With the introduction of public health measures (like water filtration, the pasteurization of milk, and vaccinations for children), mortality rates decreased. Housing was improved. Still, many unskilled workers struggled to find stable jobs and the pain of significant inequality endured.

Urbanization did enhance employment opportunities for accountants, insurance agents, and small retailers. White-collar workers emerged as a new middle class. At the same time, more young women entered the labour market, working in industry and service occupations until they got married.

During the first half of the 20th century, Black community development was closely tied to the fortunes of Black railroad employees. Thus, Black communities developed around Windsor Station in Montreal.

Because Black women were not allowed to join mainstream women's groups, such as the Canadian

Red Cross, they focused on their own groups, like the Coloured Women's Club which was established in 1902. According to Este, Sato and McKenna, in their article outlining the history of this important organization, "Club members organized several events that enabled community members to survive in an environment that was hostile to people of African descent, therefore becoming a 'pillar of strength' that fostered a stronger sense of community among Blacks living in Montreal." Through their contributions during this time period, these African-Canadian women emerged as key players in the community and as early social welfare practitioners. The women spearheaded fundraising efforts, with money raised covering the costs of medical treatment, burials, and births for community members.

In January of 1921, the porters' union was finally recognized as the Order of Sleeping Car Porters. While this unionizing effort was taking place, there was also a national campaign to end liquor sales in public places. However, Montreal's own Prohibition initiative was defeated, and the city became known as a "wet" city. As a result, jazz musicians from the northeastern United States, particularly Harlem, poured into Montreal during the 1920s. Jazz culture was the focus of many businesses in the porters' community of Saint Antoine. Musicians Oscar Peterson, Joe Sealy, Oliver Jones, and the jazz club Rockhead's Paradise all helped make Montreal one of the top jazz cities in North America. Meanwhile, the Negro Community Centre (NCC) provided spaces for young Black people to gather.

The Strengthening of a Silenced Community

Anne Rockhead met her husband Kenneth Rockhead, son of Rockhead's Paradise founder Rufus Rockhead, in her teens at one of the NCC's community forums. She was born in Montreal on August 22, 1934.

Due to the lack of access to social clubs, community centres, cinemas, restaurants, and other public places, Black children lacked social activities, making the events put on by the NCC all the more important. They included dances, movie nights, dance classes, music classes, after-school care, and much more. Anne Rockhead's good friend—jazz pianist Oliver Jones—also attended these events. Social gatherings such as these strengthened the community. Because of them, many of the children who frequented the NCC felt seen and empowered, regardless of their social condition. Even Black artists who were passing through the city understood the importance of the community centre and would give free shows there. Anne said most of the Black kids in the area went to the community centre to gather and enjoy themselves, cultivating a strong communal bond.

Rufus Nathaniel Rockhead's navigation of social class and corruption helped pave a path for the evolution of the Saint Antoine neighbourhood. Born in Jamaica around 1896, he grew up in Maroon Town where he belonged to a long line of Maroons who had fought for freedom and independence in Jamaica over centuries of enslavement. He ran a shoeshine stand before becoming a sleeping car porter for the Canadian Pacific Railway. Like Marcus Garvey, who was influenced by the Maroons, Rockhead understood the importance of self-sufficiency for himself and his community. During his eight years working the Montreal-Chicago route, Rockhead ended up smuggling bootleg liquor into the United States. While the government and the Mafia profited greatly from the sale of alcohol, Rockhead found a way to benefit as well.

He established the vibrant jazz club Rockhead's Paradise at the heart of Saint Antoine in 1928. Well-known as a nightspot in the city, the club was visited by jazz greats such as Louis Armstrong, Billie Holiday, Ella Fitzgerald, Leadbelly, Nina Simone, Fats Waller, Dizzy Gillespie, Sammy Davis Jr., and the Montrealers Oscar Peterson and Oliver Jones.

The success of Rufus Rockhead embodies the self-reliance and Pan-Africanist philosophy of Garvey's United Negro Improvement Association (UNIA)—self-reliance that the UNIA, the Negro Community Centre (NCC), and the many other organizations of Saint Antoine encouraged. While the story of Rufus Rockhead does not end here, the impact his success had on the community is most important. Anne Rockhead reminds us that, "it takes a different kind of individual even to consider that angle. But he had the foresight to make contacts and build himself a market." She understood just "how forward-thinking he was."

Meanwhile, neighbourhood folks had started to mobilize. West Indian entrepreneurs established a strong Black economic base in Saint Antoine. During World War I, immigrants from the West Indies attempted to enlist in the Canadian Expeditionary Forces but were turned away and they settled in Saint Antoine instead. Members of the West Indian community also founded the local UNIA chapter in 1919. Influenced by the politics and thought of Marcus Garvey, this organization offered a positive platform for individuals to express pride in racial heritage, history, and culture. At the height of the UNIA's influence, Black people attended Sunday services at Union Congregational Church and UNIA social activities in the afternoons. Meetings on Sundays focused on Pan-Africanism, which included lessons on UNIA philosophy and discussions about international news stories involving Black people. The UNIA's Liberty Hall—which served as a meeting place and activity centre—also offered dances, socials, and concerts each week.

A group of women from the Union United Church established the Negro Community Centre in Saint Antoine in 1927 to alleviate poverty and promote racial progress in the greater Montreal area. Social, recreational, and educational activities were offered to complement the religious and social offerings of the church.

Canadian-born Black people tended to be particularly marginalized; their lack of education and poverty meant they occupied the lowest social position among Saint Antoine's Blacks. The founders of the NCC believed that Black people should know how to fit in and how to create change from within. As a result, the Council of Social Agencies and the Financial Federation of Montreal became partners in this effort. Most current organizations in the English-speaking Black community are descendants of the NCC, UNIA, Union United Church, and the Coloured Women's Club. Additionally, Saint Antoine is the birthplace of Quebec's first Black newspaper, a credit union, and several fraternal, temperance, and independent societies.

Building Our Space

During the Great Depression, nearly 80 percent of the Black population of Saint Antoine was unemployed, resulting in outmigration to the United States. Social service providers often failed to consider the needs of Black citizens. The cause of this alienation was racist ideology that figured Black people as as slaves and servants, without land or citizenship. Consequently, Montreal's Saint Antoine neighbourhood developed its own support system.

In 1926 the Canadian Association of Social Workers was founded, with its charter members drawn mainly from child welfare agencies, municipal departments, and settlement houses. Social work agencies faced high demand during the Great Depression, but the government was reluctant to support the advancement of trained social workers.

In the early 1920s, Black organizations challenged local ordinances, provincial laws, and national policies that attempted to segregate Black Canadians. Facing diverse struggles such as chronic underfunding of schools in Black-majority neighbourhoods, Black Canadians lobbied for the opening of parks and swimming pools in their neighbourhoods and worked to desegregate seating in theatres and churches. Owners of hotels, motels, inns, and local restaurants were forced to serve Black clients following sit-ins staged by the Black community in 1944. In that same year, Ontario passed anti-racial discrimination laws, becoming a leader in human rights legislation. The rest of the provinces slowly followed suit. Saskatchewan passed the most comprehensive anti-discrimination laws in 1947, and Quebec was the last province to affirm Black Canadians' human and civil rights in 1964.

It is essential to acknowledge the role undertaken by the Negro Community Centre, the Universal Negro Improvement Association (UNIA), and the Coloured Women's Club in the Saint Antoine community (now known as Little Burgundy) in this march toward self-affirmation and inclusion.

Chapter 4

Silenced Voices: The Road Toward Recognition

Jessica Williams-Daley

French-Canadians enlisted in lower numbers than English speakers during World War II, unwilling to fight for a colonial power set on oppressing them. This created tensions between the language groups in Montreal. However, the linguistic divide was not a central issue for Blacks who desired to serve their country by joining the military.

Ironically—given that they fought against fascism in World War II—many Blacks were subjected to racism and racist policies in the Royal Canadian Air Force as well as other military sectors and organizations.

The war caused many to turn towards prayer, however Blacks were prevented from attending all-white churches at the time. The Union United Church of Montreal, one of Canada's oldest Black congregations, was one of the only places able to bring together many Black Christians.

Reverend Charles H. Este had formed the Negro Community Centre in 1927, aiming for social integration. After the war, Reverend Este as well as his church inspired great change as they worked to oppose barriers to Black enlistment in the Air Force.

Other sectors saw change after the war, too, and Black artists flourished in the jazz sector, where the most notable figure here was Oscar Peterson (called "the Brown Bomber of Boogie-Woogie" and "the Master of Swing"), who recorded his first records in Montreal. One of Canada's most honoured musicians, as well as one of the greatest jazz pianists of all time, Peterson was not the only ground-breaking musician in Montreal, as Louis Metcalf and the International Band at Café Saint-Michel became the city's first Bebop band. They were a well-known "sensation" in both English and French media, and the band was racially diverse, regarding and promoting themselves as "democracy in music." Hence, artistry triumphed over the many political, social, and military barriers Black people faced in Canada.

Covert Discrimination

Many Canadians would describe their country as a peaceful nation in which newcomers were appreciated. It is a common misconception that the United States assimilated and suppressed immigrants, but not Canada. Though Canada did not have segregation—Jim Crow—laws and other outward policies of oppression that were so characteristic of the United States. segregation did exist in Canada where discrimination was covert.

While some Canadians relish in the notion of their nation's purported moral superiority, the experiences of people of colour in this country break down this façade, as revealed in this period by the treatment of Japanese-Canadians and Black Canadians in the Royal Canadian Air Force and other military contexts.

Hidden Contributions

Black soldiers are often disregarded in Canadian war history, with their numerous contributions omitted from the story. This has left the many Black soldiers who fought for the well-being of their country with a sense of unimportance, while their white counterparts have their stories consistently told.

Black soldiers fighting in World War II, like Owen Rowe, noticed this disregard and strived to reaffirm the great contributions of Black soldiers. Rowe dedicated his final days to gathering proof of such contributions, collecting pictures and documents that displayed the lives of his fellow Black soldiers. He wanted to prove that those soldiers served, so that their stories would not be hidden, silenced, and forgotten. He wanted to commend them for their service.

Owen Rowe decided to save the stories of West Indian Black soldiers from being lost at their deaths, providing crucial facts regarding their service. His own experience was just one of the many silenced stories of Black soldiers' experiences in the Royal Canadian Air Force.

Owen Rowe's Story

Britain ordered many citizens of its colonies to defend their interests in the war, and this led to over four hundred men travelling over twenty-five hundred kilometers by land and sea to Canada. Many West Indian men (even those with no prior military training) found themselves in various Canadian provinces with the intention of serving the Empire.

Born in Barbados on May 14th, 1922, Owen Rowe departed for Montreal in May 1942, leaving behind tropical breezes, sandy beaches, and most importantly, his family. He trained with both the Royal Canadian Air Force and the Canadian Army in Canada.

Rowe and other men sailed in ships that took almost seven days to reach the New York City harbour, then journeyed to Canada by train. Upon their arrival in Montreal, they experienced culture shock and a drastic change in climate. Slushy yet crunchy white snow coated the ground beneath their feet. It was cold to the touch, a foreign, unfathomable substance that many prayed would not be present all the time. Little did they know, they would have to learn to embrace it.

The sounds of the French language flooded their ears with unfamiliar inflections. The language barrier caused many communication issues between the soldiers and the inhabitants of Montreal. They prevailed by exploring the culture of Longueuil and Montreal, tasting traditional Quebec cuisine, and visiting the city's many stores. Rowe successfully completed his personal training, thus enabling him to obtain the rank of flying officer. Fortunately, he did not recall ever experiencing overt racism during his training in Montreal. This was a unique experience, as initially the Canadian army rejected Black volunteers, with the Royal Canadian Air Force reportedly refusing to accept many qualified Black applicants as we have seen.

Rowe believed that the practice of Canadian bases not being segregated (unlike American ones) aided in the integration of all races. Living together enabled the fusion of cultures, thus allowing greater understanding of their unique differences, beliefs, values, and experiences.

However, Rowe did recall the ignorance he experienced during his time as a soldier. The N-word was used in regular parlance, as many regularly associated the term with Black individuals. Rowe noted that they were not using the word necessarily as an insult but rather as a normalized moniker for the Black race.

Following the end of the war, some Caribbean soldiers applied for Canadian citizenship; others went back home to reunite with their loved ones. Rowe returned to Barbados to see his family again, as well as his cherished friends. However, the warmth and familiarity of his home country was no match for his desire to make a life in Canada. "I'd already spent more than five years in Montreal," Rowe said, "I received a university education and settled."

Rowe did return and decided to do something with his life and the knowledge he had of the stories of Black brothers who fought to defend Canada alongside him. He decided to take on the task of providing recognition for the many Black men and women who left their homelands to train and fight for a nation that never recognized their efforts. Rowe lobbied for the Canadian government to acknowledge their contributions in order to give voice to these rich Black histories. "I want to document the Canadian-Caribbean connection in World War II and pay tribute," he explained. With Rowe's collection of many documents and photographs, he planned to showcase the stories of Black soldiers, and have their efforts properly acknowledged by the government.

Following the Second World War and culminating through the early 2000s, three hundred West Indian men and women were finally recognized for their wartime contributions to the Canadian military with a commemorative plaque unveiled at the newly opened Canadian War Museum in Ottawa, in 2005.

Marlene Jennings, the former MP for Notre-Dame-de-Grâce, stated,

As one who had the privilege to call Owen Rowe a dear friend, I am delighted that his efforts to ensure our new War Museum highlight the contributions of our WWII West Indian veterans have been successful. I was honored to have actively supported Owen in his advocacy for the recognition and it will be a moment of pride and accomplishment that is also bittersweet because Owen is no longer here to celebrate this day.

Though Rowe was unable to witness the realisation of his project after his passing on April 16th, 2005, his drive to uplift silenced voices enabled the acknowledgment of Black Canadian soldiers who defended their country.

Sad Endings

Not all stories of Black Montrealers serving their country in World War II ended in such triumph. Black soldiers like Edwin Erwin Phillips were part of a doomed mission to aid Poland after the end of the war. Born in Montreal and working as a printer's apprentice, he commenced his service with the Royal Canadian Air Force. There he obtained the rank of sergeant as a mechanic with the No. 168 Heavy Transport Squadron, sometimes accompanying transatlantic cargo flights. As there was a shortage of medical supplies in Poland, the Canadian Red Cross donated tons of penicillin towards the end of the conflict. Unfortunately, as Phillips and the four other crew members journeyed to Warsaw on a Flying Fortress, they crashed into a hilltop near Halle, Germany, and the plane burst into flames. On November 4th, 1945, those men died whilst aiding in a humanitarian crisis. Canadian participation in WWII, including that of Edwin Erwin Phillips, resulted in the safeguarding of many lives. The five crewmen were buried at Munster Heath Cemetery in Germany and were commemorated on the Canada's Air Force Poland Humanitarian Plaque.

Impactful stories like these, detailing noteworthy contributions to Canadian history, have often gone unnoticed due to discriminatory policies. Such policies will be discussed through the story of Allen Bundy and a reverend who spoke out against injustice.

Allan Bundy's Voice

Unlike Owen Rowe, Allan Bundy was one of many Black Canadians who experienced overt racism when wishing to serve his country and protect all those he held dear. Unfortunately, for the dominant society, his skin colour determined who he "truly" was, which was to say, *not* a Canadian, but rather an alien, an outsider, a Black man. His skin colour overshadowed his citizenship.

Born in Dartmouth, Nova Scotia, Bundy first tried to enlist in the Royal Canadian Air Force in 1939 at age nineteen, with his friend Soupy Campbell. Germany had just invaded Poland, prompting Canada and its allies to mobilize their militaries after declaring war on the Nazis. It was important to have as many men as possible to aid in the protection of the nation. At the Halifax recruiting centre, Bundy's application was denied, while

Campbell's was approved, even though they shared similar credentials; Soupy Campbell was a white man, whilst Bundy was Black.

Bundy believed that this was due to the recruiting officer's racist attitudes, as this was a common occurrence faced by minorities in World War I (Bundy's own father served in Canada's only all-Black unit, the No. 2 Construction Battalion). Though Bundy was rejected, he was still determined to join the Air Force.

Beneath the discrimination faced by minorities at the recruitment centre, an unpublicized policy was quietly preventing Black and Asian Canadians from attaining all but general positions in the entire RCAF as well as the Royal Canadian Navy. The RCAF's Colour Line policy of 1939, required that all volunteers had to be "British subjects and of pure European descent." Regardless of how long Black Canadians had lived in Canada, or how recently they had emigrated from the British West Indies or elsewhere in the Empire, they were still barred as not being of "pure European descent."

Allan Bundy knew his self-worth and ignored all notices under the National Resources Mobilization Act, which called for a national registration of eligible men, and authorized conscription for home defence a few years later, causing an RCMP officer to visit his home. When questioned about his refusal to act upon the notices, Bundy said, "I had gone to join the Air Force in 1939 and if the bullet that kills me is not good enough for the Air Force, then it's not good enough for the army, either."

Shortly after this encounter, Bundy went back to the Halifax recruiting station in 1942 to try again, as there was a new commanding officer stationed there. In the end, Bundy became one of the very few Black Canadians to be accepted for aircrew training. He was stationed in Ontario as part of the British Commonwealth Air Training Plan, and joined 404 Squadron in 1944, but it was still not good enough for his white counterparts. White navigators refused to fly with him despite his great ability as a multi-engine pilot. However, a white sergeant by the name of Edward "Lefty" Wright agreed to fly with him, leading to great wins for Canada. For instance, on October 15, 1944, they helped sink the 426-ton German Auxiliary Trawler VP.1605 Mosel and the 1202-ton Norwegian tanker Inger Johanne off the coast of Norway. Together, they flew forty-two more missions before the end of World War II.

Black Revolutionaries

The incredible stories of Owen Rowe, Edwin Erwin Phillips, and Allan Bundy showcase the varied experiences of Black Canadian soldiers, as well as the many contributions each made to their country.

Owen Rowe flourished in a multicultural battalion and managed to include the unique perspectives of West Indian soldiers into the fabric of Canadian history. He had their wartime efforts acknowledged both nationally, in the Canadian War Museum, and internationally.

Allan Bundy, with numerous other Black Canadians who served with the Royal Canadian Air Force during the Second World War, was credited by the Canadian War Museum for having helped "change attitudes toward visible minorities in the military, and in Canadian society."

Edwin Erwin Phillips was a part of an effort to aid a population in need and died an honourable death doing so. However, his story is not widely known. The suppression of Black stories is the concealment of history. It is imperative to acknowledge that Black stories have immense value in Canadian history, and that we have a right to be heard and understood in all media. This is what Owen Rowe fought for, Allan Bundy countered, and what Phillips suffered after his death.

Challenging a Racist Policy

The Black Canadian community consistently challenged barriers regarding their admission in the armed forces, as well as the refusal to include Black experiences in the historical record. Reverend Dr. Charles H. Este of the Union United Church of Montreal was a driving figure in pinpointing the barriers to enlistment of Black Canadians in the Air Force.

In May 1941, Reverend Este received an unsigned letter written on behalf of National Defence Minister J. L. Ralston, stating that there were "no barrier[s] to the enlistment of a Negro in certain categories in the Air Force." They characterized Reverend Este's followers— the Black community—as his "people," and stated that "many opportunities will be given to them to serve in [their] united cause." Already the divisive nature of such a letter showcased the concealed stigma against Black people, as the minister attempted to evade charges of racial discrimination.

A Budding Musical Style

Artistic developments in wartime had their own impact when the Bebop (or simply Bop) style of modern jazz was born in New York City in the early 1940s and ultimately split jazz into opposing camps. The new style was characterized by using the chromatic scale (twelve notes) rather than the diatonic scale (seven notes) of earlier jazz. It also allowed drummers to speed up as they played, with many solos played in double time, rather than the previous slower metronomic regularity. Hence, jazz soloists had more freedom when improvising. The greats who started this movement include alto saxophonist Charlie "Bird" Parker, pianist Thelonious Monk, trumpeter Dizzy Gillespie, drummer Kenny Clarke, and guitarist Charlie Christian.

Montreal-born Oscar Peterson, who had studied classical piano with Paul de Marky, a Hungarian concert pianist, won a $250 cash prize from the Canadian Broadcasting Corporation (CBC) national music competition in 1940, at the age of 14, and was on his way to stardom.

The Maharaja of the Keyboard

Dazzling audiences with his skill and the swift yet precise movements of his fingers on the piano, Peterson soon launched his own weekly radio show, *Fifteen Minutes' Piano Rambling*, on the Montreal radio station CKAC. His radio fame spread rapidly, going national by 1945 on the CBC's *Light Up and Listen* as well as *The Happy Gang*.

Still a teenager, he got offers from musical greats like Jimmie Lunceford and even Count Basie to join their bands in the United States. Peterson's father, who did not want to allow his son to leave school to pursue a musical career, reportedly told him, "If you're going to go out there and be a piano player, don't just be another one. Be the best." Oscar did just that. He was a celebrity on the music scene in Montreal by this time and did drop out of high school to play as a featured soloist in Johnny Holmes' dance band in 1943. He also created his first recordings for RCA Victor in March 1945. His recordings of songs like "I Got Rhythm" and "The Sheik of Araby" revealed his talents in Boogie-Woogie music, which earned him the nickname "the Brown Bomber of Boogie-Woogie."

Louis Metcalf, a prominent American jazz trumpeter who arrived in Montreal in December 1945, created the city's very first Bebop band, composed of seven individuals. Metcalf believed that his group represented "democracy in music" as they came from diverse ethnic and racial backgrounds. The band was consistently featured in both the English- and French-speaking press and played in the legendary Café Saint-Michel for about ten years, cementing their role as central figures in Montreal's jazz community.

The World War II had lasting effects on Black Montreal, intensifying long-standing tensions between English and French-speakers and increasing language-based discrimination against Black communities. Many Black Montrealers faced conscription and compelled to fight in an overtly racist Canadian army. In strife, however, they found solace. The war prompted an influx of Black migration and the need for community. Montreal became home to several Black-led and -created community organizations and social bodies, as well as cultural hubs, and Black creativity, art, and talent flooded the streets of Montreal's Saint Antoine district, painting the city with an incredibly rich legacy.

Chapter 5

Early Immigration and the Rise of the Black Diaspora

Renee White

The aftermath of World War II was characterized by significant changes in Quebec society. In Montreal, a growing number of middle-class French speakers were entering the professional work force. This postwar era saw the beginning of the baby boom as well as an increase in income and spending. Suburban areas were expanding, which created the need for better transportation. This led to the construction of new highways and the development of public transit systems. The economic prosperity that arose after World War II was in part due to Canada's social and economic linkages with the United States, and demand for Canadian resources.

In determining the factors that gave rise to the Black Canadian diaspora in the fifties, it is important to explore the economic conditions that existed at the time. The Great Depression had been characterized by unemployment, low income, and decreasing prices. It left citizens exposed to the hardships that came along with poverty. Most families struggled to keep afloat. Many were forced to rely on government aid. Throughout these times, the importance of social welfare, the concept of social security, and the need for better financial support emerged.

After World War II, the American demand for Canadian raw materials and consumer goods increased and more jobs became available, which helped improve Canadian economic conditions. To maintain this growth, Canada needed to expand its labour force. This was also essential in order to increase tax revenues and support better social welfare programs.

The aim was to get immigrants specifically from Europe, which at the time had thousands of refugees and displaced persons. Ultimately this also influenced Canada's social structure as it gave room to a new wave of immigrants, which meant fewer Canadians of British descent.

The liberalization of immigration laws in the early sixties reflected a move toward tolerance, equality, and the development of a more demographically diverse state. On the other hand, considering the limitations to economic opportunities for migrant workers, the idea of opening immigration to other nations also had within it an element of opportunism. Laws and policies were actively used to deny Blacks and other people of colour entry into the country, with women being specifically targeted based on the assumption that immigrant women would increase immigrant populations.

The continuous misrepresentation of Black people as inferior and incapable of contributing to civilization negated the chances of Blacks benefiting equally from socio-economic mobility.

Negro Citizenship Organization

One of the monumental figures in the fight to end racist immigration laws was Donald Willard Moore, a Black Canadian civil rights activist. He founded the Negro

Citizenship Association (NCA) in 1951, which aimed to change preconceived notions about Black people. As the president of the NCA, he engaged with the Department of Citizenship and Immigration on its restrictive policies. It was believed that people from the Caribbean could not assimilate to Canadian culture because of the harsh weather. Mr. Moore was able to challenge these stereotypes and show how Black people had historically helped to shape Canada. It was through this debate that Canada opened its doors to Black people, beginning with the West Indian Domestic Scheme in 1955.

The NCA was pivotal in supporting members of Montreal's Black community by challenging discriminatory practices. Richard Leslie, a Sir George Williams University alumnus from Barbados, later took on the presidency of the NCA, where he aimed to increase awareness of the organization's objectives and gain allies. Under Mr. Leslie's presidency, the NCA stood up against the Queen Elizabeth Hotel in a legal battle where a Black applicant was denied employment due to the position allegedly being filled, only for it to be offered to a white applicant a few days later. The case was brought to the Supreme Court, where the hotel was found guilty and fined.

The NCA was also integral in breaking down systemic barriers that pervaded Montreal's taxi industry. Prior to the late 1960s there was only one taxi company— called Veteran's Taxi— that employed Black people as required by the government. Both Diamond and LaSalle taxi companies only employed white drivers. Through Mr. Leslie's perseverance in pursuing this issue, he was able to pave the way for other Black people to become taxi drivers, utilizing his qualifications to obtain his own taxi permit and later gain employment with both Diamond and LaSalle taxi companies.

The Domestic Scheme

The West Indian Domestic Scheme came into effect in 1955, eventually allowing nearly three thousand women from the Caribbean to enter Canada as domestic workers. While initially only a hundred women were allowed, it became increasingly popular, and many more were able to come to Canada through this program. The domestic program allowed 580 women from the Caribbean to come to Montreal between 1955 and 1961. Despite their qualifications, many worked as domestics for years before they were able to enter other fields.

The intention was that Caribbean women would work for one year, after which they would be granted immigrant status. Once they remained in the country for five years they could apply for Canadian citizenship.

The program helped facilitate relations between Canada and Caribbean countries and, at the same time, worked to fill domestic labour shortages as more Canadian-born women began to enter the labour market. Though it opened the door for Black Caribbean women to enter Canada, it was not without limits. The women that were selected went through invasive medical examinations and had to meet specific criteria to be selected to come to Canada. Many of the women were subjected to harsh working conditions, toiling for long hours in white households where they suffered discriminatory treatment. When, subsequently, they were able to search for other jobs, they were discriminated against in the job market.

When they did find employment, they were paid less than white workers. Furthermore, given their vulnerable immigration status, they could not formally attest to the discrimination they faced as their status remained directly in the hands of their employers. Thus, most had no choice but to acquiesce.

While the program is known to have helped contribute to employment of (low-skilled) Black women within the Black diaspora, it should be noted that many of the women were highly educated and came from middle-class families, leaving jobs in their home countries with hopes of creating better lives for themselves in Canada.

Racial Tension

The notion that Blacks could only come as domestic servants suggests that white Canada retained attitudes derived from earlier days of plantation politics and the transatlantic slave trade, reinforcing a racial hierarchy that reinforcing a racial hiarachy where Black people remain at the bottom. The exploitation of Blacks and exclusion of better integration in Canada reveals much about the nation's supposed tolerance. The apparent act of tolerance was less about being progressive and more about opportunism, reinforcing white supremacy. For example, at a time when more white Canadian women were entering the labour force, their previous constrained roles were expected to be filled by Black women, showing the social status of the Black diaspora in Canada.

The idea that racism is an inevitable occurrence given the presence of so many different cultures in one place was a common misconception. Though it is important to note that while diversity can create tension, that tension does not equate to racism. Racism allows one group to be in a superior position by sustaining more privileges than others. Prior to 1967, immigration was open to two types of immigrants. White immigrants, who were considered ideal, and then people of colour. In 1967 the labour market shifted with the rise of new technologies. The previous demand for immigrant workers shifted to workers with specialized skills. Together, with the evolution of populations, this led to a massive change in immigration laws. Canada had no choice but to increase its diversity to meet the needs of the new market.

Black diaspora immigration was shaped by racial capitalism, which normalized discrimination and inequality. The history of unequal treatment and colonialism created huge disparities in wealth worldwide, and yet is normalized. With an evolving immigration policy and the need for economic balance, Canadian identity would transform from all white to multiethnic/multicultural. Though Canadian nationality was slowly changing, belonging was still far removed from the Black experience. According to Henry et al:

> Multiculturalism as ideology has provided a veneer for liberal-pluralist discourse, in which democratic values such as individualism, tolerance, and equality are espoused and supported, without altering the core of the common culture or ensuring the rights of racialized and Indigenous peoples.

The concept of Canadian citizenship was stable for whites, but in the Black community, citizenship was partial and easily revoked through deportation.

The Point System

When the domestic scheme ended, immigration shifted to a points system. This was aimed at reducing discrimination by allowing entry based on skills, education, and other specialized qualifications regardless of race or ethnicity. It allowed immigrants from more countries access to Canadian citizenship. However, it also disadvantaged other countries by enticing their highly skilled workers away, especially countries with far fewer resources.

Despite the emphasis on being non-discriminatory, the points-based system persisted in being overtly discriminatory. The visa process, for example, further marginalized less-developed countries. While some countries had multiple visa offices, other countries with higher populations of people of colour had fewer visa offices, often only one. Preferred countries had quicker processing times, whereas others had much slower processing times, with vague or confusing paperwork. Some countries which previously had not required a visa, now did. This was the case, for example, in Jamaica.

In this new immigration system, white people were still the preferred race. Furthermore, it was more difficult for Black and other migrant women to gain entry through the points system. Many educated women from the Caribbean could only get through as domestic workers even long after the domestic scheme ended. Canada's system, supposedly based on merit, nevertheless still benefited the dominant cultural group, further pushing people of colour to the margins.

Moreover, this system promoted class disparities, as people who could afford to accumulate points through the specified criteria could be candidates, though people who could not afford such luxuries were not given the same opportunity. The points-based system meant that only those who fit capitalist Eurocentric criteria were eligible, and even when those individuals did get selected, they endured the jobs that whites refused to do.

Jazz

As has been discussed, Montreal's Saint Antoine neighbourhood was heavily occupied by Blacks from the diaspora in the 20th century. With high racial tensions, it was difficult for people of colour to move to other areas, as many landlords were reluctant to rent to them. The marginalization of Black people also resulted in low incomes, and a significant reduction in their mobility. Eventually, with labour mobility due to shortages, and the rise of less restrictive immigration laws, the Black Quebec diaspora was able to expand to other spaces in the city.

The need for more inclusive places came as a result of not being accepted into white spaces. Many nightclubs refused entrance to Black musicians and guests. This gave rise to nightclubs catering to the Black community. Although Montreal has the reputation of being more tolerant than other places, Black people were still often excluded from public spaces. The growing popularity of nightclubs in the city that hosted jazz musicians not only brought representations of Blackness into cultural spaces but also laid the foundation for Black resistance against the status quo. The opportunities created from having inclusive spaces not only helped to create Black mobility but also supported a sense of identity and belonging.

In the fifties, nightclubs quickly grew in popularity, becoming sources not only of community but of inspiration and employment for many musicians. Jazz played a role in developing the Black diaspora in Montreal and was also a form of self-expression.

Jazz was not warmly received at first by white Montrealers, as it was a musical form connected to Black culture. Nightclubs were places where Black people could go to release the day's tension, creating an environment of community and belonging, uniting folks with entertainment and live music. Among the famous nightclubs for jazz musicians and Black visitors were Rockhead's Paradise and Café Saint-Michel on Saint Antoine Street. Aldo's was also a popular choice, located on Mountain Street in the 1950s. Aldo's stayed open twenty-four seven, had its own chef, and not only employed musicians but functioned as a place for them to socialize and enjoy each other's performances. Café Saint-Michel was popular for hosting Louis Metcalf and the International Band, while Rockhead's Paradise was famous for having quality performances. Its owner, Rufus Rockhead, of Jamaican heritage, was known for always showing great hospitality to guests.

Rockhead had been able to provide employment during difficult times in the Depression era. He went out of his way to hire as many people from the Black community as he could. He supported the Black community in a way the government could not. Because systemic barriers kept Black people socially, economically, and politically oppressed, it was important to have safe spaces like Rockhead's Paradise that could foster Black talent in the community.

The professionalism and musical virtuosity displayed in these nightclubs attracted tourists from the United States. Many musicians and bands came to Montreal and played in the city. They helped strengthen the Black community economically, and the talent curated in Montreal nightclubs was recognized as far away as New York City. It was during the golden era of the fifties that jobs for musicians were plentiful, and the jazz community thrived like never before. Black musicians from the United States were attracted to the strong jazz scene in Montreal, where they were able to support themselves and live comfortably as jazz artists.

Local Montreal Jazz musicians were inspired by Oscar Peterson. They wanted to expand their careers to New York and be known abroad. Oscar Peterson, being from Montreal and known internationally, was a beacon of success. He inspired many to fulfill their dreams as jazz artists, though not everyone would have the same successes or opportunities. The strict immigration policies of the US limited the development of their careers.

Along with the growing popularity of nightclubs in the city came organized crime. Gang members were heavily affiliated with nightclubs, though musicians often did not participate in the violence and gang activity. Indeed, their very lives were at risk being connected with nightclubs that hosted gang members. In 1954 things began to change when Mayor Jean Drapeau was elected. His plans included ridding the city of crime. For Drapeau, that meant dissolving the nightclub scene, which would have a serious impact on the city's jazz community. Furthermore, it was during this time that many more people began investing in television, so fewer people felt inclined to spend money on nightclubs. As time progressed, jazz declined, and rock'n'roll slowly took over.

Though Jean Drapeau's goal was to eradicate crime, it cannot be ignored that his anti-vice campaign directly interfered with Black culture. Not only did jazz circulate in nightclubs, but it was also commonly associated with the Black community. As noted by scholar Robyn Maynard, "the practice of publicly associating Black life and Black independence with crime and danger has an enduring legacy that continues to impact Black mobility." The cleanup diminished crime operations, but at what cost?

Conclusion

The aftermath of the Great Depression had a lasting effect that continued into the early 1950s. This was a turbulent time, characterized by severe economic changes as communities experienced poverty and the dislocation of the Second World War.

It was also during this time that nightclubs began to gain traction in Montreal. This created many opportunities for musicians to find work and so began the golden era of jazz in Montreal. The city's jazz scene drew immigrants from the US. Canada's Domestic Scheme, established in 1955, allowed an influx of women from the West Indies to gain citizenship in Canada. As the city's Black diaspora began to rise, Black people started to face evictions in what came to be known as Little Burgundy. Organizations like the Negro Citizenship Association (NCA) worked to combat discriminatory immigration laws.

Chapter 6

They Came, They Saw, They Wanted Change

Amanda Georgina Ghartey Asomani-Nyarko

When you think of Black power and other forms of political activism in the 1960s, Canada ranks among countries that experienced relatively peaceful and constitutional change, as opposed to the visibility, radicalism, and frequent violence attending the protests associated with the civil rights movement south of the border from 1954 to 1969.

Canada was a settler colony with significant constitutional and legal ties to the United Kingdom up until the repatriation of the Constitution in 1982. Moreover, the small size of Canada's minority populations, as well as the relative absence of Jim Crowism or a plantation economy made it easy for certain anti-Black perspectives and ideas to cross the border from the US. In fact, many Canadians deny that racial discrimination exists in Canada. Both Canadian and Quebec history tend to focus on the battle for land between French and English settlers, and the brutal exclusion and actual physical elimination of Indigenous peoples.

Discussions of discrimination in Canada and in particular Quebec are usually in connection with language rights and protections and their implications. But Canada and Quebec have a history of slavery, violence, and racism that has been neglected or excluded from the formal teaching of our history. So, whenever you walk the streets of Montreal, Black figures are hidden in the shadows. From your favourite café on Notre Dame Street to Old Montreal, from the streets of Little Burgundy to the ninth floor of Concordia University, they were there. Black Canadians and English-speaking West Indians have engaged in struggle with the European settler classes in Montreal since long before the 1960s. These struggles increased in intensity and gained momentum within Black communities with the birth of the Black power movement in the US.

This chapter seeks to explore the activism and the various societal shifts occurring in Montreal during the sixties that influenced the creation and evolution of Black spaces by Montreal's English West Indian communities. It will first look at the emergence of various associations and groups in the mid-fifties and early sixties such as the Jamaica Association of Montreal (1962), Trinidad and Tobago Association (1964), Saint Vincent and Grenadines Association (1965), Caribbean Conference Committee (1965), and Guyana Cultural Association of Montreal (1967). These associations and groups allowed newcomers to maintain their cultural identities while building communal ties and a sense of belonging in Montreal.

It will then examine the latter half of the sixties, where Black power concepts, a revival of the Black American renaissance, Garveyism, and Pan-Africanism became more prominent as Montreal's West Indian communities endeavoured to create an identity and to integrate more fully into Montreal society.

To accomplish these objectives, Black intellectuals and community leaders held two influential conferences in 1968. One group, the Caribbean Conference Committee, under the chairmanship of Professor Clarence Bayne and in collaboration with Dorothy Wills (a masters graduate social worker at the time), organized the conference held at Sir George Williams October 4th–6th, 1968. The conference sought to explore the "problems of Involvement in Canadian Society, with reference to the Black Peoples." The second group, a pan-Black, pro-Marxist and Black power collective, held the notable Congress of Black Writers at McGill University, also in October 1968. A group of resident Caribbean students created the Quebec Board of Black Educators (1968).

Bayne points to the fact that it is generally noted that at the Black Writers' Congress, none of the speakers were women. And only one, Rocky Jones from Nova Scotia, was born in Canada. Moreover, there was no link between the event and the students' occupation of Concordia and the crisis that took place there following the two conferences. In fact, says Bayne, the initial congress conference visionaries, Conrad Franklyn and Sammy Boldon, had resigned from that conference group because of what they considered to be a radicalization and takeover of the agenda of the event by Rosie Douglas and his supporters. Moreover, the Caribbean Conference Committee which Bayne chaired declined to organize a workshop at the congress to discuss Canadian issues, stating that Canadian racism and local Black integration problems were too important to be reduced to a mere workshop. He pointed out that the push for solidarity between Montreal's fragmented Black communities had reached a peak during the latter half of the sixties, awakened by events very independent of the Black Writers' congress or the Sir George Williams Affair (1968).

These events led to the creation of the National Black Coalition of Canada (1969) and La Ligue des Noirs (1969). This chapter addresses both the internal and external forces such as covert and overt racism that plagued the lives of English-speaking Black immigrants, forcing them to create associations explicitly tailored to their needs, which later pushed for the solidarity of Black people in Montreal and across the diaspora. Indeed, the sixties is when we see Black activism at its finest.

New Immigration Laws

In the 1960s there was a massive influx of Black immigrants from English-speaking colonies to Canada. Quebec, especially the island of Montreal, received significant numbers of these immigrants. Prior to the sixties, Montreal had a small Black population; it increased dramatically due to changes in immigration laws in the 1960s.

Canada was not always seen as a welcoming country to immigrants of non-European ancestry. It was only starting in the mid-fifties that Canada began to open its doors to non-whites. In the last fifty years, multiculturalism became the strategy for building the Canadian state, at the core of its social and political values.

Following the genocide of the Second World War, there was an awakening worldwide to issues of racial discrimination. In 1960, Prime Minister John Diefenbaker introduced the Bill of Rights, which frowned upon any discrimination based on skin colour, nationality, religion, or gender. These changes made it more difficult to limit the immigration of racialized persons.

The Conservative Party came to power in Canada in 1957 at a time when the unemployment rate was extremely high. There was also growing concern about the influx of immigrants who were unskilled and could become unemployed. These were predominantly white immigrants, who despite being unskilled, were sponsored by their relatives. There was a need for labourers possessing technical and professional skills. What better way to tackle this growing need for skills and increasing employment gap than by opening Canadian doors to immigrants from other parts of the world? Prime Minister Diefenbaker introduced a bill in 1960 that transformed the immigration act to attract skilled workers from non-European Commonwealth countries.

Prior to 1962, Canada's immigration regulations were overtly racist and discriminatory, often rejecting people on the basis of class, race, ethnicity, religion, and disabilities. It is well documented that the people deemed desirable for Canadian society were of Anglo-Saxon ethnic backgrounds from Britain and the United States. For instance, in May 1947 Prime Minister Mackenzie King outlined Canada's immigration policy before the House of Commons as follows:

> The policy of the government is to foster the growth of the population of Canada by the encouragement of immigration. The government will seek by legislation, regulation, and vigorous administration, to ensure the careful selection and permanent settlement of such numbers of immigrants as can be advantageously absorbed

> in our national economy. It is a matter of domestic policy [...]. The people of Canada do not wish because of mass immigration to make a fundamental alteration in the character of our population. Large scale immigration from the Orient would change the fundamental composition of the Canadian population.

The "careful selection" Prime Minister Mackenzie King was referring to was defined in the Immigration Act of 1953 and Immigration Regulations of 1954 and was used until 1962.

In 1962, Ellen Fairclough, the minister of Citizenship and Immigration, introduced new regulations that eliminated the openly racist criteria. Skills became the main basis for determining who would be granted access. The new regulations established two important things: (1) non-sponsored immigrants would be evaluated by their education, training, skills, or other special qualifications and not their race; and (2) all Canadian citizens or permanent residents (regardless of where they were born) could sponsor a parent, grandparent, husband, wife, fiancé/e or unmarried son or daughter under twenty-one. However, only Canadians from certain nations in Europe and the Americas, and certain countries in the Middle East, were allowed to sponsor children over twenty-one. This clause was added due to a fear of unskilled sponsored relatives from Asian nations.

The policy was introduced not as an act, but as a set of regulations. New regulations could be implemented quickly, whereas acts had to pass through many different stages of approval in Parliament.

In 1967, a points system was introduced to rank potential immigrants for eligibility. Race, colour, and nationality were not factors in the new system; rather, work skills, education levels, language ability (French or English), and family connections became the main considerations in deciding who could immigrate. Therefore, with the arrival of tens of thousands of immigrants, mainly from the English-speaking Caribbean and the United States, the Black community remained largely English-speaking.

Between 1961 and 2001, the Black population in Canada increased substantially. In 1961 the Black population was 32,100, making Blacks 0.2 percent of the population. By 2001, the numbers increased to 662,200, making Blacks 2.2 percent of the population. In fact, Black people in Canada make up the largest of visible minority groups. In 2001, Toronto had the largest Black population in Canada (310,500), with Montreal (139,300) ranking second. According to Winks, "West Indian migration increased rapidly. In 1946–50 there had been 947 black arrivals, or 0.22 percent of the total number of immigrants; for 1961–65 there were 11,835, or 2.37 percent of the total; and by 1966 blacks— largely West Indian—comprised over 3 percent of all immigration."

The Emergence of West Indian Associations

In the face of systemic anti-Black racism, hate, and racial oppression, Black and other visible minority immigrants needed to forge communal bonds. They required a safe space to discuss issues of racism in the Canadian context, colonialism in their homelands, and corrective strategies like those of the Black power movement.

In Montreal, such Black spaces are provided by the Jamaica Association of Montreal (JAM), the Trinidad and Tobago Association (T&T Association), the Saint Vincent and Grenadines Association (SVGA), the Guyanese Cultural Association of Montreal (GCAOM), and the many others shown in the map presented in the introduction. These groups emerged throughout the sixties, and their purpose was to provide members of their respective communities with resources and support in Montreal. They represented early Black activism in Montreal and were highly influential in debates surrounding Black power in the Canadian context.

While the Island and Black diaspora agencies tended to organize themselves in country-of-origin subgroups, their struggles to reduce the restrictions of the colour line have enhanced and improved the lives of all English-speaking Black Montrealers, regardless of their backgrounds. Paul Hébert points to this when he recognizes that the associations played a critical role in the parliamentary commission on immigrants, where they advocated against Canada's racist immigration policies. They were highly influential in founding the National Black Coalition of Canada (NBCC).

This section will focus on the origins of these associations, their role in integrating and promoting West Indian culture in Montreal, and the move to solidarity of all the associations. This will illustrate how the racism faced by immigrants upon arrival sparked the creation of these groups and revealed early Black power in Montreal.

Can you imagine arriving in a foreign land, excited for the opportunities that await, but upon arrival, you are met with racial hostility? In this place, there are not many people that look like you, and you are searching for something that reminds you of home. This was the reality that many Black and other visible minorities faced upon their arrival in Canada in the mid-fifties and early sixties. They needed to feel a sense of belonging in a city that othered them, and the associations played a crucial role in fulfilling this need.

For instance, in an interview conducted with Sharon Nelson, the current first vice president of the JAM, she mentions how it started as a social club in a small space on Van Horne Avenue, a neighbourhood full of immigrants where people would get together and find themselves. Dr. Clarence Bayne, one of the founders of the T&T Association, echoes this when he asserts that the association was founded in Arthur Goddard's basement apartment at 550 Milton Street, where young Black people gathered to socialize. Jack Dear, the current president of the SVGA, expresses the same when he mentions that the seeds of the SVGA started as social meetings in members' basements and homes between 1961 and 1962, before its establishment in 1965. GCAOM's current secretary, Pamela Richmond, says that in 1966, several Guyanese had an idea to get together and unite all Guyanese in Montreal. Indeed, through socializing in the homes of young and charismatic West Indians, they helped one another cope with their new reality. These interactions allowed them to keep strong ties with their homelands while assisting newcomers of their exact origins.

While the core activity of these associations was to create a sense of community and belonging, the prominence of their early activism for Montreal's Black communities should not be overlooked. To combat the social, political, and economic issues that many Caribbean immigrants faced upon their arrival in Montreal, many of these associations acted and still act as an integration service for West Indian newcomers. From the 1960s until the 1980s, Jamaica was the leading source of Black immigrants in Canada, making up 30 to 40 percent of all immigrants. After the change in immigration regulations in 1964, the flow of Jamaicans to Canada dramatically increased—until then there were not more than a hundred Jamaicans entering Canada each year. John Maxwell shows the increase in numbers as follows: 1965: 1,214; 1966: 1,407; 1967: 3,459; 1968: 2,885; 1969: 3,889.

Many Jamaicans were leaving the Island to find better educational or employment opportunities (as was the case for many other Islands at the time). In fact, many Jamaicans migrated to the UK between 1948 and 1971, and once Canada began opening its borders to non-white migrants, Jamaicans made the most of the opportunity. With so many Jamaican immigrants coming into Canada—their top destinations being Toronto and Montreal—Montreal's small Black community grew dramatically.

To respond to the growing Jamaican population, the JAM bought a building in the Côte-des-Neiges area. This space allowed people to bring forth their complaints, which were then forwarded to the appropriate organizations. This was crucial considering how scattered Montreal's Black community was. Having a known space created a sense of solidarity amongst Black folks.

Similarly, the SVGA focused on creating a smooth transition for Vincentians upon arrival. Between 1955 and 1967, the West Indian Domestic Scheme brought about three thousand women from the West Indies to Canada to work as domestic servants. To be eligible, women had to be single, between the ages of eighteen and thirty-five, have at least an eighth-grade education, and pass a medical examination done by Canadian immigration officials.

These women's expectations were not met upon entering Canada. In fact, they were paid less than they anticipated and were required to work longer hours. After a year of domestic work, they were granted landed immigrant status and could seek educational and employment opportunities in other fields. They were also permitted to sponsor a family members' permanent residency in Canada, which the Canadian government tried to limit by only accepting single women. After five years in the country, the women became eligible for Canadian citizenship.

Bigger cities, such as Montreal and Toronto, were popular immigration hubs for many of these women. For instance, between 1955 and 1961, 580 of 1,600 women chose to work in Montreal. Many Black women were victims of racial discrimination and hostility when arriving in Canada, and Montreal was no different.

Few had never worked as domestics before migrating, and many did not plan to continue working in the domestic field. Jack Dear, current president of the SVGM, who was active in the sixties, asserts that, "some of [the women] had problems with the mistresses and would seek help from the association, who would intervene and try to settle the issues." Likewise, Pamela Richmond mentions how the GCAOM and other associations allowed domestic workers to meet with one another and share their experiences, so they no longer felt alone. The immigrants' struggles with racism spurred the growth of the organizations.

Due to the racist ideology embedded in Canadian society, many Blacks had trouble renting apartments. It is true that Montreal did not have Jim Crow laws like our neighbours south of the border. However, Montrealers chose to segregate themselves in the absence of any legal determinant. This was an aspect of Canadian society for which many Black immigrants could not prepare. Bukka Reine, an immigrant from Trinidad and Tobago and one of the original complainants during the Sir George Williams Affair, said, "it seems to me that Canadians are racist, but they like to apologize for being racist."

Many immigrants expected Canada to be a friendly and accepting place. However, this was not the reality they experienced. For example, according to Hébert,

> In 1961, a McGill fraternity refused to rent a room to a Jamaican student and, according to the West Indian Society, then called campus housing services to request they only refer "Canadians and Americans" looking for rooms. Two weeks later, a day after the *Star* had praised McGill's climate of "racial harmony," *Star* journalist and Jamaican-Canadian activist Alvin Johnson revealed that McGill's housing services allowed landlords to exclude renters on racial grounds. Three years later, after a leasing agent assured a Sir George student

that there were "no n--s" in the apartment building he was considering, the Georgian sent two Black students to inquire about an apartment. They were quoted a rent of $115 and told no apartments were available for three months. The paper then sent two white students who were told that an apartment was available immediately for $110.

Traditionally, Montrealers had very limited experiences with Black residents, and Blacks could not hide their Blackness like other immigrants could hide their origins, causing West Indians (and other Blacks) to be met with racial hostility and discrimination by white Canadians. For many of the associations, the safeguarding and promotion of Caribbean culture was essential in breaking down the colour line. This was true for the T&T Association, GCAOM, SVGA, and JAM.

Dr. Clarence Bayne recalls that in 1964, McGill University hosted a cultural evening for international week. Roosevelt "Rosie" Douglas, the late prime minister of Dominica and an activist during the Sir George Williams Affair, did a performance of the limbo dance. He explains that at the time, there were many different versions of the limbo dance. There was the limbo as ritual performance, limbo as cultural entertainment, and what Black power advocates called "house n**** limbo for tourist entertainment." In the latter, the principal dancer might dress like the "American 'Darkie,'" a character that developed from the racist culture of blackface. The outfit consisted of a straw hat and tight-fitting three-quarter-length pants showing the extensions and dimensions of certain body parts, with red patches on the pants. The dancer is also bare-chested, barefoot, wide-eyed, grinning with white teeth showing, and gyrating.

Soon after the McGill cultural event, students joined Bayne and others at Goddard's home. They expressed their feelings about what had taken place. Some even described Rosie's presentation as "a tourist-pleasing misrepresentation of the limbo." They described it as being disrespectful of Caribbean and African cultures.

The group's consensus was that "this African thing" had served as an instrument of self-preservation and resistance against the oppression of colonialism, and that such forms of culture and history needed to be presented with care and pride. The group concluded that they must be the gatekeepers of their culture. They must take charge of how they were seen, understood, and defined in Montreal. They must take the same pride in how these elements of their culture were presented as other ethnic groups were doing at the time. On that evening in 1964, the T&T Association was born.

It's important to note that the T&T Association was expected to eventually evolve and dissolve. They planned to have leadership that was very global in its vision and comprised very independent-thinking university types. They proposed to establish numerous programs that would later stand on their own. They argued that the Trinidad and Tobago Association was a short-term tactic to bring about the longer-term objective of creating a more unified Caribbean community—which it did.

Bayne and his colleague Arthur Goddard were committed to writing the association's constitution. Their aims and objectives were defined as the following:

(a) To create the climate and facilities necessary for fostering a dynamic West Indian community in accordance with the Canadian concept of nationhood based on harmonious cultural diversification.

(b) To attain the ultimate reality of a unified West Indian community in which a strong West Indian Culture capable of contributing to ensuring a variety of Canadian culture is achieved.

These objectives led to the transformation of the association's Drama Committee into the Black Theatre Workshop (see Chapter 8). The T&T Association was central to the creation of the West Indian House and was an active supporter in the creation of the Quebec Board of Black Educators. This commitment to unification also made it possible for the association to play a leading role in the creation of the National Black Coalition of Canada (NBCC).

Similarly, the GCAOM was birthed out of the need to promote and maintain Guyanese culture and to foster relations among Guyanese and non-Guyanese in Montreal. Guyana is a unique country. It has substantial African and Indian communities, and although it is situated in South America, much of its culture and many traditions are adopted from the Caribbean. Guyana is the only country in South America that was colonized by the British and the only English-speaking country in South America. Therefore, it is no surprise that Guyanese sought to protect and maintain their culture in Montreal where many other groups were doing so at the time.

In July 2020, the Caribbean Coalition Network of Montreal was formed to combat the dispersion of

Montreal's English-speaking communities. It comprises the Jamaica Association of Montreal, Saint Vincent and Grenadines Association, Guyana Cultural Association of Montreal, Barbados House Montreal, Grenada Nationals Association of Montreal, Antigua and Barbuda Association of Montreal, and the Dominica Island Cultural Association of Montreal. All the presidents of the English-speaking West Indian associations meet monthly to discuss how they can work together and unite West Indians throughout Montreal. This is critical, now more than ever, with English minorities being further marginalized with Quebec's Bill 96. Although West Indian associations cater to the needs of those from their homelands and ethnic backgrounds, their efforts to combat anti-Black racism have positively impacted all Blacks. The rationale here is that yes, we are West Indian, but anti-Black racism has no limits. Anti-Black racism is not just going to stop because you identify yourself as Jamaican or Haitian. Blacks are not a monolith and have different cultures and practices. Therefore, they must consult with one another and offer a hand any time one of us is in need.

In an interview, Jack Dear expressed that there had been many attempts to bring the Islands together, and he's happy to see that this group is holding up. When asked why it has taken so long for the associations to create this united front, Pamela Richmond said, "Personally, and this is just my opinion. [...] We as human beings, [...] always want to be the one up front. And it takes [...] a very special people to get together and say, okay, you are just as important as I am. [...] Until you're at that level, there's going to be a problem."

This relationship between the associations is promising because each has something unique to bring to the table. For instance, the JAM has a physical building that allows them to be proactive rather than reactive. Ultimately, by advocating for Jamaicans, they have become a representative of the Black community in Montreal. But this is something that the organization should not carry alone. Each of the historic Black English-speaking associations that emerged throughout the mid- to late-20th century brings something to the table to generate wealth in the community. This coalition should not come as a surprise, as Montreal is the city for Black unity and power conferences.

Montreal as the City of Black Power Conferences

In the mid- and late-sixties, Montreal became the focal point for notable Black power conferences that were mainly organized by the West Indian community. As we have seen in previous chapters, Black folks in the city were gathering and meeting long before the sixties, and it would be unjust to assume that Montreal's Black communities only got organized with the arrival of West Indians. However, the native-born Black community was inconspicuous and very dispersed in the late sixties due to the urban renewal of Saint Antoine, which at that point was beginning to be referred to as Little Burgundy. It has been shown that by 1966, Little Burgundy, which had housed 90 percent of the city's Black residents, was now home to only 2 percent of all Black people living in Montreal. This drastically affected Black community organizations such as the Universal Negro Improvement Association (UNIA) and the Negro Community Centre (NCC). Historian Dorothy Williams illustrates that the first major phase of this urban renewal started with the UNIA being moved to Notre Dame Street (where it remains today) and the government claiming its property against the wishes of the Black community, to be used for the benefit of the overall public. It was troubling that many Blacks were settling outside of Little Burgundy, in neighbourhoods such as Côte-des-Neiges, Lasalle, and Notre-Dame-de-Grâce (NDG).

Although the NCC mandate had been island-wide since 1956, the centre could not withstand the loss of Black residents in the area; the sense of community that once existed in Little Burgundy was shattered. Thus, the disbanding of Montreal's English-speaking Black communities (native-born Blacks, African Americans, and West Indians) created an opportunity for a group of West Indian individuals to start anew.

Many West Indians found themselves in Montreal with the mission of bettering their homeland. Many leapt at the chance for higher education and employment opportunities that their Island could not afford them. For many, the goal was to save their coins or pursue higher education and return home. This was true for a group of students, mainly from the Caribbean, that mostly attended Sir George Williams and McGill University.

The students formed several groups and were exposed to many influences over the years 1950 to 1970. In the late fifties and early sixties, the group at McGill promoted programs that would keep Black students in touch with Caribbean and other diasporic affairs to make for a smooth transition back into their homeland upon completing their university degrees.

On the other hand, there were students who had graduated and—along with immigrants arriving under the more liberated immigration laws—become more integrated into Canadian society, adopting Canadian lifestyles. They had formed communities outside of the university and created a range of organizations to meet their social, cultural, political, and community needs.

Over time, a debate evolved between these two groups about the merits of returning to one's country after graduation as opposed to residing in Canada or elsewhere. This difference of opinion gave rise to organizations with quite different interests and purposes, and, in some cases, inter-group conflict. In the early sixties, many of the Caribbean students at McGill and Sir George Williams were more concerned with giving back to their country of birth or making socio-economic and political changes that would improve their homelands. Others were attracted to the Canadian landscape for a complex set of reasons. Notwithstanding this divide, members of both groups brought with them a great spirit of revolt against oppression and inequality which would later transform the landscape of Black identity in Montreal and elsewhere.

There was the New World Group at McGill led by Professor Kari Levitt, who worked in collaboration with the Caribbean-led group represented by Lloyd Best of Trinidad and the University of the West Indies (UWI). They wanted to change the social and economic structures of the world so that it worked better, by radically revising the principles and laws of traditional economics and social development. Then there was the back-to-the-homeland group, the West

Indian Affairs group of McGill. They emphasized the "give-back" principle, aimed at transforming and improving efficiency and development by replacing absentee and colonial capitalist governance with local rule. Then there were the anti-capitalism and social economy or communism subgroups. They came under the influence of C.L.R. James and other activists adhering to diverse forms of Marxist-oriented scientific communism.

The student movements initially operated independently of local Black organizations in the communities surrounding the universities. Montrealers were engaged in the struggle against the colour line that they faced daily: anti-Black Racism in housing, education, employment, health services, in the churches, the hotels, the taxi services—in all walks of their lives. These barriers to Black development were reflected in abnormally low native-born Black enrolment at the universities. Very few Blacks born in Quebec graduated from local educational institutions. Black students enrolled at these universities were foreign students from the Caribbean, Africa, America, and other Black diasporic countries.

From our current perspective, Montreal appears to be an unusual place for Black power conferences. Surely, a conference on the affairs of West Indians would be more likely in Great Britain because of the high numbers of Blacks that immigrated there. However, many West Indians found themselves in Montreal due to the lifting of certain immigration restrictions. Not to mention that Montreal was home to a vast number of Black Canadians and African Americans.

Montreal therefore became the perfect place for intellectual debates regarding the state of the Black diaspora. Throughout the mid- and late-sixties, notable conferences occurred such as the annual Conference on West Indian Affairs held by the Caribbean Conference Committee (CCC) from 1965 to 1966, and the Congress of Black Writers in 1968.

Caribbean Conference Committee

Three years before the creation of the Caribbean Conference Committee (CCC), the failure of the Federation of the West Indies in May 1962 weighed on the minds of many West Indians who were in favour of federalism. For Trinidad and Jamaica, federalism opened doors for independence and a breakaway from colonialism. On the other hand, for smaller Islands, which had not yet attained self-government, it looked promising for "custom unions and economic development and functional cooperation."

For many complex reasons, the federation failed, but in August 1962, both Jamaica and Trinidad gained independence from British rule. Many of the other Islands wished to follow in their footsteps. This common aspiration to combat colonialism in the West Indies brought a group of Caribbean men and women together in Montreal. Among this group were Anne Cools, Roosevelt ("Rosie") Douglas, Franklyn Harvey, Antony Hill, Robert Hill, Alvin Johnson, Hugh O'Neile, and Alfie Roberts. The group was named the Caribbean Conference Committee and was extensively committed not only to the pursuit of West Indian unity but to providing a platform for Black intellectuals to discuss anti-colonial ideas and promote political and social change. The group's activities also had the effect of essentially reviving Pan-Caribbeanism. They became engaged in finding solutions to the discrimination and racism that the rapidly increasing Black populations of Canada were facing.

The "Triple C" worked closely with notable radical West Indian writers such as George Lamming of Barbados, Lloyd Best of Trinidad, and C.L.R. James of Trinidad. James held private classes on Marxism and liberation with the CCC members. Lloyd Best and George Lamming worked with them in the publication of the *New World Quarterly,* a West-Indian based journal of political economy.

The New World Group met on a regular basis off campus at Levitt's home. The group's co-leader, Lloyd Best, emphasized a reconstruction of the existing system based on scholarly research. The New World Group complemented the work of the CCC. For instance, in 1966, New World asked George Lamming to produce a special issue for its journal *New World Quarterly* on Guyana's independence. Lamming, who had ties with the CCC, called on the group to assist in preparing the journal.

New World Quarterly was more than just a journal. It provided young West Indian intellectuals from all different backgrounds—whether they were historians, poets, literary critics, economists, political scientists, sociologists, or journalists—a platform. *New World Quarterly* comprised mostly academics (mainly economists) who were engaged in research on social and economic issues, whereas the CCC was primarily a political organization comprising Caribbean students. Therefore, these groups were not in competition with each other. In fact, the two groups had a similar goal of freeing the Caribbean from colonialism and focused on creating post-colonial Caribbean societies. According to David Austin, Dany Fougères, and Roderick MacLeod, this 1966 prospectus published in *New World Quarterly* best describes the CCC's mission:

> The purpose of the 1966 Conference will be to discover in ourselves, in our societies, the roots of West Indian freedom. From being the historical agent of other interests and peoples, the West Indian has for over three centuries been seeking to make his own history. To know what that history has meant to our forebears and what it means to us today, what have been its defeats, triumphs, and manifestations—that is the responsibility of the present time.

This was significant because in the past, meetings about the West Indies always had the theme of international charity, as if the Islands were incapable of standing on their own. The intention of this meeting was different. It was not about leaders or subordinates. It was simply a desire for West Indians to meet with each other. With four Caribbean countries—Jamaica, Trinidad and Tobago, Barbados, and Guyana—becoming independent by 1966, such conversations were necessary to shape and further understand West Indian identity.

The CCC was instrumental in planning a series of annual conferences between 1965 and 1967. The first conference on West Indian affairs took place on

October 8th and 9th, 1965 at the University of Montreal. Many West Indians from Canada and the United States attended. The meeting was called "Shaping the Future of the West Indies."

The second conference took place on July 6th–8th, 1966, and was titled "The Making of the Caribbean People." It argued that historically West Indians had been alienated from their society and unable to analyze their situation on their own terms. "For the first time," according to Hébert, it was West Indians who were "thinking seriously" about the region, as opposed to the past when "the thinking about ourselves was done by others."

The conference ended on a note that stressed the importance of unity and independence as essential tools for true West Indian sovereignty. The speakers argued that the "harsh fact" facing West Indians was that their "survival and freedom [would] depend on [their] independent activity as a united people." Prominent figures contributed to the overall theme of the evening. Frances Henry of McGill University and Mervyn Alleyne of the University of the West Indies discussed "Race and Culture in the West Indies"; Dr. Hugh Waker, a West Indian employed by the provincial government of Manitoba, and Bernard Yankey of the University of Wisconsin, spoke on "Economic Change and West Indian Development"; and Locksley Edmondson of the University of Waterloo and Alvin Johnson of McGill dealt with "Politics and Change in the West Indies."

The ideas that Caribbean Blacks needed to speak for themselves and work to solve their problems as a united people resonated with oppressed peoples worldwide. It was not only a reality of the West Indian students studying at university. It was also a reality for Black citizens born in Canada and Quebec. It was reflected in the activities of the Coloured Women's Club; the NCC and its outreach programs; the activities of the UNIA and the local Garveyites; the Jamaica Association, the T&T Association, and its vigorous support of Black theatre; the creation of the West Indian House; and the Quebec Board of Black Educators. The difference is that the Caribbean Conference Committee for West Indian Affairs was about Black life external to the Canadian social and political biosphere, whereas this concurrent awakening was about Blacks living in Canada.

After its third and final conference in 1967, the Triple C dissolved and many of its members became dispersed. However, a few became interested in Black nationalism. They knew that if Canada was going to be their home that things needed to change, not only for them, but for future Black generations. To further actualize this shift in thought, the Caribbean Conference Committee became the Canadian Conference Committee. Historian David Austin describes this shift as the "passing of the torch from the older generation to the newer generation." This gave birth to the notable Congress of Black Writers that took place on Canadian soil, on the island of Montreal.

The Congress of Black Writers

The year 1968 was eventful, with demonstrations worldwide, and Montreal was no exception. Protests were common. There were rising tensions between Montreal's English speakers and the French-speaking majority; women's groups were advocating for their rights; students were protesting, and there were many other groups fighting for their seat at table. The small island of Montreal was enraptured with big ideas of liberation and decolonization.

With the murder of the world's biggest dreamer and strongest advocate of nonviolence, Dr. Martin Luther King Jr., on April 4th, 1968, many from all different walks of life took to the streets of Montreal to express their sorrow. Like how the death of George Floyd in June 2020 was the catalyst for an awakening about systemic anti-Black racism and a cause for sorrow worldwide, Dr. King's death pulled on heartstrings globally. Many felt hopeless as they tried to endure the fact that the King of Love, the King of Possibility, the King of Freedom was murdered. If the world's most peaceful man could be murdered in cold blood for standing up for oppressed voices, then what hope was left for humanity?

On the other hand, his death sparked an awakening for Blacks on an international scale; many pledged to carry on his dream and the city of Montreal was a flashpoint for all these emotions and ideas of freedom. This was the political climate and scenery of the Black writers' congress.

The Congress of Black Writers was a four-day conference held at the Student Union Building of McGill University from October 11th–14th, 1968. It is known as the largest Black power conference outside of the United States. It was dedicated to MLK and Malcolm X, two prominent leaders for Black liberation. The conference was the embodiment of the shift in ideology regarding the Black situation in Canada and abroad, representing Black power in the Canadian context at its peak.

At this point, West Indians began to view Montreal and Canada as their homes, and their attention was less focused on their homelands. The conference brought together some of the world's most charismatic and intellectual Blacks all in one room. C.L.R. James, Stokely Carmichael, and Walter Rodney were among the featured speakers. According to David Austin, Stokely Carmichael's speech was the high point of the conference, leaving many emotional, as Carmichael "emphasized the importance of focusing on oppression as a system, proclaiming that 'revolution is the total destruction of the old system—total destruction—the re-emplacement of a new system which speaks for the masses of the people of a given country."

Austin also points to the fact that the congress had two major implications for Canadian society. The first one was that Black people were mobilizing to take their seat at the table, and the second was that anti-Black racism existed in Canada. Dr. Bayne had this to say about the conference:

> What we have left from the Congress is a debate that will be remembered for the will to continue the struggle for full and total liberation. What the conference at Sir George left was the will to fight on with reference to the problems of Blacks in the Canadian situation; but as M.C. Curdy admonished, in solidarity with Blacks not only in Canada, but elsewhere, especially Blacks in the USA.

Having such notable conferences taking place in the small city of Montreal generated solidarity amongst Black communities.

The Quebec Board of Black Educators (QBBE) also focused less on the Islands and more on Canadian society.

The Quebec Board of Black Educators

During the 1960s, Canadian education underwent various expansions and reorganizations. In Quebec, there were two different types of private and public schools: Protestant and Catholic. This is reflective of the historical and religious ties of British and French settlers. Protestant schools were mainly for English speakers, while Catholic schools were for French speakers. The Quebec school system was already fragile due to the complex nature of this bifurcated structure. Half of all Quebec students were leaving school by the age of fifteen, one of the highest high school dropout rates in Canada.

In response to this, between 1961 and 1964, the Royal Commission of Inquiry on Education in Quebec recommended the adoption of new academic methods and the creation of bodies such as the Ministry of Education (which removed the authority over schools from churches), comprehensive schools, CEGEPs, and the Université du Quebec network. By 1966, the Quebec school system was better equipped to handle the high dropout rates and the commission announced the creation of fifty-five Catholic and nine Protestant school boards.

By 1970, Quebec's secondary school enrolments doubled because it became mandatory for children to be in school until the age of fifteen. While the implementation of the commission's recommendations could be seen as a success for Quebecers, it failed to address the cultural differences between (1) Quebec's white English-speaking and French-speaking communities and (2) the province's Black and other visible minorities, who were dramatically increasing in population and were also attending these schools.

Many West Indian immigrants began establishing themselves and their families in Montreal. With the increase in Blacks and other visible minorities, there came the realization that Quebec's school system was racially biased and not culturally inclusive. The teachers could not properly meet the needs of Black children born in Canada. They were either unable or unwilling to adapt their teaching methods to fit the needs of Black children. Many Black and other visible minorities felt alienated in Quebec schools, and as a result, very few racialized students pursued higher education.

It is noteworthy that the thirst for knowledge and pursuit of higher education has always been important to Black communities. For centuries members of the Black diaspora have been forbidden to pursue basic education such as reading and writing due to the slave trade and colonization. To many Blacks, education is the cornerstone of the effort to achieve equality, independence, and prosperity. Through extensive research done by Black scholars from Montreal's top four universities (McGill, Sir George Williams, Loyola, and the University of Montreal), it became clear that there was anti-Black racism embedded in the school system that was preventing Black students from completing high school and pursuing higher education.

It soon became evident to members of the Black community that there needed to be a group of Black individuals who could remedy the problems that affected the education of Black youth. These problems included the low expectations of Black youth, discouraging guidance counsellors, and issues relating to proper integration. According to Gilbert Brathwaite, such a group would speak to the issues of "personal acts of discrimination by white teachers against Black children" and set up mechanisms to alleviate the trauma experienced by Black children who had been barred from academic streams and "condemned to the wasteland of practical courses." This group would take steps to prevent such situations from arising in the first place.

In response to the educational and societal needs of English-speaking Black communities, a group of concerned Black educators (namely, Clarence Bayne, Leo Bertley, Oswald Downes, Garvin Jeffers, Ivy Jennings, Roosevelt Williams, Marion Lowe-McLean, and Mary Robertson), mainly from the Caribbean, came together and founded the Quebec Board of Black Educators (QBBE) in 1968. The organization was legally recognized on December 29th, 1971, and Leo Bertley was the leader of the group.

From its creation in 1968, the QBBE became very influential in advocating for and actualizing its goal of serving the educational needs of Quebec's growing Black communities. More recently, it has extended its mission to include other visible minorities. Their current mission statement is:

> To encourage and support continuous improvements in the education system of Quebec and the equitable distribution of its benefits to communities of colour, such that the programs will provide the best opportunity to pursue educational attainment which in turn will impact social and economic achievements.

What makes the QBBE so influential, from the mid-20th century to the present, is the fact that it was created by Blacks and tailored specifically to the educational and societal needs of that community. Its structure, goals, initiatives, and programs were ahead of its time, and it has continued to cater not only to the needs not only of Blacks, but also those of other visible minorities. Its revolutionary essence can be seen in its most prominent innovations and programs including the DaCosta Hall Summer School, the BANA Program, and the 17 Point Agreement, which shall be discussed here.

The DaCosta Hall Program

The DaCosta Hall Program was created in 1970 and was initially organized by Black students who attended McGill University. It was originally called "Across the Halls" and its purpose was to improve the educational performance of at-risk Black high school students and afford them the opportunity to complete required courses to gain admission to McGill, Sir George Williams, as well as the CEGEPs.

For the 1969–70 school year, McGill University admitted that there were only fifteen African Canadian students enrolled at all levels of study. This was problematic, considering the Black population in Montreal was substantially growing and there was an increase of native-born Black Canadians. Black communities under the leadership of the QBBE connected this tiny number of Black McGill students to the high dropout rate in Montreal high schools, and the million-dollar question was: why are so many native-born Black Canadians dropping out of high school?

Something needed to be done. Black communities knew that the city of Montreal was rapidly changing, and many other groups were also fighting for their seat at the table, most notably French Canadians with the Quiet Revolution. They knew that only they could provide the necessary tools to change this intentional flaw in the school system. Through extensive research and meetings, the QBBE was able to secure a one-time contribution of $12,000 from McGill University to the Across the Halls Program (now known as the DaCosta Hall Program). McGill agreed to accept twenty of the ninety students in the summer program. As a result, in the 1970 Fall semester, McGill admitted fourteen students (unfortunately the other six students could not afford the tuition).

Essentially, the DaCosta Hall Program started as an initiative to work alongside the formal education system until the problems surrounding Black youth in the school system were eliminated. It then blossomed into a permanent summer program of the QBBE that Black and other minorities still take advantage of today. Currently, students enrolled in the DaCosta Hall Program can obtain credits accepted by the English Montreal School Board (EMSB). Students can also write the Quebec Ministry of Education (MEQ) supplementary exams and attain credits.

Its structure had an administrative unit which consisted of a principal, secretary, assistant secretary, and volunteer general assistant. "The principal was the chief administrator of the project, while the secretary and assistant performed several supportive tasks. The volunteer functioned both as a student supervisor between classes and as a substitute teacher."

Today, the purpose and goals of the DaCosta Program remain the same as in 1970: to provide students at the grade eleven level with sufficient academic credits to be admitted to university, to instill a sense of Black pride and identity in the students as motivation for their success through life, and to begin the enrichment of Black students' education from grades eight to ten so that they could be moved from the practical to the academic stream.

According to Bayne and Bayne, the program's uniqueness "derives from the fact that the personal development of the individual was one of [its] main focuses." Baron Lewers, an immigrant from Jamaica, took advantage of the program for two summers in the eighties. He recalls it as something he looked forward to, even though he went to a more distant high school, and he also recalls the teachers as pleasant and "willing to teach you." Seeing that they were only teaching five to six courses, lasting twenty to thirty minutes each, the teachers had additional time for explication. This is a highly important feature of the program, filling some of the gaps in the Western educational system, which is a by-product of colonization. Specifically in the Canadian context, Eurocentric pedagogy leaves out equally important information about Black history, Indigenous history, and people of colour (i.e., the BIPOC context).

Although in Montreal at the time there was no law that explicitly demanded segregation, Montrealers carved out the city in ways that segregated its inhabitants, which created an "us versus them" dichotomy. So, when Black Canadians were sent to predominately white schools, they were othered, both racially and culturally.

In education, students are viewed as subordinates. But Blacks are often dehumanized even further, with pedagogy in Quebec viewing Black children as less than, representing them in "Black" roles such as being a porter or working in the homes of white people. This only further emphasized the need for such a support program.

Even now, anti-Black racism is still embedded in our school system, for example, the provincial curriculum does not recognize Canada or Quebec's involvement in the transatlantic slave trade, and Canadian Black history is still relegated to the back burner. The DaCosta Hall Program allows students to view their teachers as equals and nurturers, preparing them to reach their full potential in an anti-Black, white supremacist world. This contributed to the success of the program, which, in partnership with the BANA Program, has assisted over fifteen thousand students since 1968.

The BANA Program

The BANA Program started in 1972 through the initiative of QBBE member Garvin Jeffers, its founder and creator. The program gets its name from the Swahili word meaning child. While like the DaCosta Hall Program, it was created to meet the academic and cultural needs of Black elementary school students. The rationale of the QBBE at the time was that if the problems Black youth were facing were caught at an earlier stage in their development, then the program would no longer be needed at the secondary level. The problems would have been alleviated and a sense of Black pride and identity instilled in the children.

The BANA Program was created to act more as a preventative than a short-term remedial solution. When it started, it lasted six weeks and was split into academic and recreational sections, and it was always presented from a Black perspective. The QBBE and the Black Community Council of Quebec (BCCQ) operated the BANA project. Both groups agreed that the QBBE would handle the academic component, while the BCCQ would operate the recreational element.

To make such a program possible, Garvin Jeffers secured a grant from the Protestant School Board of Greater Montreal (PSBGM) and Vanier College in 1972. Currently, most of the funding comes from the QBBE itself, as well as a grant from the Ministry of Education. The goals of the program were, and still are, to motivate Black students to learn, and to return a confident Black child to the formal school system—goals that are not as concrete and measurable as those of the DaCosta Hall Program. The point of the program from its inception has been to instill a sense of Black pride and identity in younger children with the goal of it carrying on into their adolescence and adulthood.

What made the BANA Program special is that it provided children with Black role models and had the children engage in activities highlighting their culture and history. Again, this illustrates how the QBBE was ahead of its time; the group knew how important representation was, especially for Black children. They gave Black youth and other visible minorities the opportunity to learn from people who looked like them and could understand them as individuals. This is very important, considering Black history and culture were not at the forefront in the traditional school system.

Additionally, the BANA program is unique due to its community-based collaboration. For instance, many community groups contributed to the program, such as the Côte-des-Neiges Black Community Association, which supplied the personnel to coordinate the recreational component.

Today the BANA Program is available for young kids at the elementary level to take advantage of during the summer. As described on the QBBE website, the summer school curriculum consists of early intervention in literacy and numeracy in the morning, and sports, cultural, and arts activities in the afternoon. Math, science, English, and French make up the academic courses in the morning, while the history of Blacks, arts and crafts, physical education, and cultural field trips are activities planned for the afternoon. The BANA Program continues to contribute to the lives of BIPOC in the twenty-first century. Importantly, the program catered to the needs of Blacks and other minorities through the 17 Point Agreement, which we shall now discuss.

The 17 Point Agreement

On November 29th, 1970, the QBBE, under a special committee, conducted a study regarding the problems of Black students, after which they drafted and presented a document to the PSBGM called the "17 Point Agreement." This document cemented the relationship between the PSBGM and the QBBE and outlined the major issues that the QBBE were concerned with.

Other Black organizations attempted to provide education for Blacks outside of the traditional school system. The QBBE felt that the formal education system was responsible for providing proper education for everyone, including Blacks. If the formal education system wanted to disregard Blacks, the QBBE made it their duty to put mechanisms in place to ensure that Black children's needs were met, nonetheless. According to Braithwaite, on April 27th, 1971, the PSBGM adopted the seventeen recommendations of the committee.

The recommendations were:

1. The Board (PSBGM) appoint an experienced Black teacher to act as a liaison officer between the Black community and the elementary schools.

2. An experienced Black social worker be appointed to the Social Work Department.

3. The services of a Black psychiatrist or psychologist to be obtained to do the testing of Black students who are being considered for placement in special classes.

4. The board make every effort to recruit a greater number of qualified Black teachers the elementary level.

5. The Curriculum Council be requested to establish a committee to prepare a Black studies programme. Upon the approval of the Department of Education, this programme would be introduced into the schools as credit courses and would be open to all students.

6. Wherever possible, Black studies programmes be handled by Black teachers.

7. In schools where there is no Black studies programme Black literature and Black

History be incorporated with the regular school curriculum.

8. A Black Studies programme be offered in the evening schools, if and when Black Studies are offered, as credit courses.

9. Textbooks and records with racial bias (especially at the elementary level), if they exist, be replaced.

10. More books written by Black people be made available in school libraries (elementary and high).

11. A bibliography of Black studies be made available to all schools.

12. Black guidance teachers to be made available to guide Black students in the high schools and that those counselors be placed in given schools and be made available to Black students at large.

13. These guidance teachers be responsible for recommending the initial placement of Black high school students from within the system, and a table of equivalence be worked out between West Indies, British and Canadian systems, with particular regard to grade level.

14. Remedial and adjustment services for Black students be made available where required and that Black teachers be appointed to operate these services where possible.

15. Black students to be given the opportunity to opt out of present standardized tests of mental ability, if their parents so request.

16. An ad hoc committee consisting of the liaison officer (proposed in recommendation No. 1), the principal and the district superintendent be established whenever there is a conflict regarding placement or some other problem. Further, that the parents of the child involved be automatically invited to attend the meetings of the committee.

17. The committee to be given a mandate to continue in operation until an ad hoc committee be established in conformity with recommendation No. 16.

These recommendations put out clear guidelines as to what Blacks were expecting from the education system. It has been proven that pursuing an education while Black, especially in predominantly white spaces, is not always the greatest experience due to a lack of representation amongst teachers, racial discrimination in the classroom, and the anxiety felt when learning about topics surrounding Blackness which are not always depicted accurately, or are overlooked. These are some of the topics that we will cover in the next section of this chapter with the Sir George Williams Affair of 1969.

The Sir George Williams Affair

We've ambled the halls of the Henry F. Hall Building at Concordia University many times before. We recall seeing diverse groups of students with different accents working and socializing together. We've always admired and loved the diversity inside the university but have never experienced this diversity in the classroom. We felt a sense of anxiety on the sixth floor when a white professor uttered the N-word in a class lecture. But never had we made our way up to the ninth floor of the building until we sat down to write this chapter.

The ninth floor of the Henry F. Hall Building should be considered a historical landmark. It embodies the screams, cries, and courage of Black students and their allies who fought for fairness in the school system. The event that endowed the building with infamy made international headlines echoing what many already knew about Canada: that covert and overt racism existed at all levels of society.

The event that changed the landscape of Montreal forever, and by extension, the scenery of Canada, was the "Sir George Williams Affair." Many scholars have called the Sir George Williams Affair—the most significant uprising led by students in Canadian history—a riot. Now more than ever, language is important, and words hold power. When Black people are fighting for their basic human rights, it is perceived by the white majority as "violent" or "disruptive." A riot is an extremely violent disturbance. We refuse to call this event a riot. "Affair," "crisis," or "uprising" are more appropriate to describe the events that occurred between January 2nd and February 11th, 1969.

A look at the scenery of Montreal during the second half of the sixties is crucial to understanding the Sir George Williams Affair as a phenomenon. Intense intellectual conferences that involved Black people across the diaspora—such as the previously mentioned

Caribbean Conference Committee of 1965 and the Congress of Black Writers in 1968—foreshadowed the students' protests. Blacks in Montreal were ravished with ideas of Black power and liberation. At this point, the West Indian communities were searching for their identity as self-determined people and began to see themselves not only as West Indians but also as Canadians. These intellectual debates, intertwined with the spiritual nature of demonstrations in Montreal, contributed to an overall Black Renaissance that climaxed in the events of the Sir George Williams uprising.

Contrary to popular belief, the Sir George Williams Affair did not happen all at once. It was not simply a group of violent students wanting to disrupt the peace; the students sought to balance the scales of justice and erase the colour line. Before turning into a series of explosive events on February 11th, 1969, the roots of the Sir George Williams crisis can be found in April of 1968.

Six Black students from the Caribbean—Terrance Ballantyne, Allan Brown, Kennedy Fredericks, Wendal Goodin, Rodney John, and Douglas Mossop—filed a complaint of racial discrimination and incompetence against their biology professor, Perry Anderson, with the dean of students, Magnus Flynn. Anderson was distributing failing marks to all Black students in his class, regardless of the quality of their work. In the words of Rodney John, "none of us were failing students, just failing students in Anderson's class."

In an interview conducted with Dr. Dorothy Wills, who was very active in the community and supported them throughout their protests, she explained that "[Anderson] graded them and had a marker and would cross out the grade of the marker's numbers and said he is the professor, and he could do what he wants." She also added that Anderson referred to Black students as "miss and mister, and when asked why he did this his reply was, 'I could be having a beer with any one of these kids in the class, but not with you.'" Terrance Ballantyne, one of the original complainants, echoes this account of microaggressions when he recalls that Anderson referred to him and other Black students as "miss" and "mister" and referred to white students by their given names. Ballantyne said that to test their theory of racial discrimination, he copied his White peers' assignments and still received a failing mark, while his white peers passed with flying colours. This made many of the students feel uncomfortable. Dr. Wills reiterates this point when she expresses why she and other members of the Black community supported the students: "Many [Black students] had experiences with professors that was not nice. I supported them because I remember being at McGill and getting grades that I didn't think reflected my work."

Therefore, with the feeling of discomfort, and Black power and liberation bruning in their hearts, the students took the proper steps by filing a complaint with the dean of students to correct the racial discrimination they faced. The university administration ignored the seriousness of the complaint and took no further action to investigate the matter.

It was not until eight months later, on December 5th, 1968, that the university and the students reached an agreement for a hearing committee to be established. The members of the hearing committee were supposed to be unanimously appointed by all three parties involved (the university, Anderson, and the students). However, the university chose to act by itself, and appointed a hearing committee and informed the students to appear on January 26th, 1969. The students refused, as this was not what they had agreed upon. They declared this to be "unconstitutional, unethical, and an act of bad faith on the part of the university."

The claimants decided to attend the hearing. However, the blatant disregard of their valid claims led them and two hundred other students to walk out of the hearings in the Hall Building auditorium. They marched their way up to the Computer Centre on the ninth floor on January 29th, 1969. Nine days later they occupied the faculty lounge on the seventh floor. While they occupied the Computer Centre, they had tremendous support within the university, the Black community, and other oppressed groups. Dr. Wills mentioned that "people from the community including me, would cook at home, and bring pots of food down to the students for them to eat. Their favourite was fried chicken or curry chicken. And we would sit together and eat together and talk about what was going on. And it was a very nice, pleasant, peaceful atmosphere." While the Computer Centre was occupied, the students made a list of five demands:

1) That the hearing committee and its subsequent proceedings be totally and publicly rejected.

2) That the administration arrange a meeting of themselves, Prof. Anderson, and ourselves to settle the composition of a hearing committee, the procedures under which any such hearing

will be conducted, and the date and time of such a hearing.

3) That any such meeting with the administration be held in an atmosphere free of all threats of reprisals and other punitive measures, juridical, educational, or otherwise.

4) That due consideration be given to those Caribbean students who have lost study time due to their brotherly devotion to this case over the last few months.

5) That all criminal charges against all Black

students be dropped immediately.

According to *UHURU*, a Black Montreal newspaper run mostly by West Indians, on February 9th, the students' and administration's lawyers came to a compromise agreement. The students signed the agreement and were assured by the university's lawyer and the dean of students that the acting principal would also sign. Many of them prepared to evacuate, and they believed that they had won a small victory, until they realized that the university pretended to be on their side to stall again, as the University Faculty Association rejected the document. According to the article entitled "Computer Centre Incident":

> Less than a hundred students were left in the building later that night, when the whole negoti-ated agreement crumbled at the last minute. The remaining protestors barricaded the stairwells on the seventh floor and shut off the elevators and telephones. They threatened to destroy the

computers if the police were called in, but the university had already turned the whole matter over to the police.

It was on February 11th at 2:00 am in the morning that Dr. Dorothy Wills got a phone call from activist Anne Cools, who told her, in her strong Bajan accent, "Dorothy, you better get down here right away, because all hell is breaking loose." Police officers arrested ninety-seven unarmed students. Many recall students throwing objects out the windows, seeing white paper fall out of the sky like snow. Moreover, many witnessed the gruesome violence that Black students faced at the hands of those who are there "to serve and protect," as well as hearing Montrealers chant, "Burn, N-words burn" and "Let those N-words burn" while a fire burned in the building. Furthermore, not even twenty-four hours after what occurred at the university, Perry Anderson was reinstated and "on June 30 that year, the hearing committee reported 'there was nothing in the evidence (before them) to substantiate a general charge of racism' and found him not guilty of racism towards the six complainants."

The words that white Montrealers chanted illustrate how rooted anti-Black racism was, and why it was important for Blacks to act if they wished to see any changes. The aftermath of the Sir George Williams crisis really had Blacks thinking about their place in Canadian society. The Black press was instrumental in reporting accurate coverage about what was happening in Montreal and allowed for constant communication between North America and the Caribbean. In fact, many demonstrations took place in the West Indies in support of the students and to condemn the attitudes of the university and the Canadian government. On the other hand, public opinion in Canada and elsewhere was not on the side of the students. The media essentially butchered the names of these young intellectual Black West Indians and denounced them as "rampaging criminals," "thugs," and "anarchists." The media blamed the loosening of immigration laws that allowed "troublemaking" students from the West Indies to attend Canadian universities.

Rosie Douglas and Anne Cools were named the ringleaders of the incident. Rosie, who was not even a student at Concordia at the time, and who was in fact a recent graduate of McGill University, served two years in prison and was labelled a "terrorist threat" by the Canadian government. He was deported back to Dominica in 1975. Years later he returned to Canada, where he received a political science degree from McGill University. Anne Cools was sentenced to six months in prison, charged with "wilful obstruction," and received a $1,500 fine. She was pardoned in 1981 and in 1984 became the first Black person appointed a senator. Rosie Douglas went on to become the prime minister of Dominica in 2000.

The events that took place on the ninth floor of the university forced administrators to re-evaluate their internal procedures. According to the *UHURU* article, "Computer Centre Incident,"

> In April 1971 Sir George Williams adopted University Regulations on Rights and Responsibilities, and the Ombuds Office was established. By December 1977, Concordia

University approved a university-wide Code of Conduct and new terms of reference for the Ombuds Office.

The National Black Coalition of Canada

Shortly after the Sir George Williams Affair, in 1969 the National Black Coalition of Canada (NBCC) was formed. It became the representative of forty-six organizations from coast to coast. Regarding the first-ever conference of Black leaders from all regions of Canada coming together to discuss their problems as Blacks, Dr. Howard McCurdy, the president-to-be of the proposed coalition, said:

> Black power involves a second thing of which I hope this meeting is the beginning in this Country—namely solidarity....at this conference, it is of particular significance that we are not only bringing together Canadian-born Blacks with Black immigrants, but it is being done by West Indian-born Blacks. We are establishing a solidarity in this Country, and I think we ought to give attention also to establishing solidarity with the Black man in the United States.

Indeed, it was Dr. Howard McCurdy who, in the words of Dr. Dorothy Wills, "lit a fire under everybody's feet." McCurdy, like many, was tired of the divide in the Black community between West Indians and Canadian-born Blacks. Dr. Wills recalls him saying, "that's a pack of nonsense... because when they see you come in, they see a Black person, they don't see a PhD. They don't see anything other than another Black person."

Forming the NBCC was not an easy task, but it was necessary to provide a voice for Blacks and other visible minorities in Canada, as well as foster relations between Afro-Caribbean and native-born Blacks. There was quite a divide between these groups. At the time, the Canadian-born Black community was very dispersed, and mostly segregated from white Canadians. After the events at Concordia a couple months earlier, it became even more apparent that Blacks in Montreal needed to unite as one people.

The NBCC made their mission clear in a document entitled "Entrenchment of the Bill of Rights in the Canadian Constitution." The organization was "dedicated to protecting and advancing the rights of Black people in Canada." It was the first Canadian national civil rights group to address barriers in housing, employment, and education that Blacks faced. Its aims and objectives were,

I. To ensure that the Black people of Canada achieve full social, cultural, political, and economic participation in the shaping of a humane society, and that Blacks benefit fully from this society.

II. To eradicate all forms of discrimination in Canadian society.

III. To foster communication and a spirit of solidarity among Blacks in Canada regardless of national origin.

IV. To foster communication and cooperation with Blacks of other nations in matters of common interest.

V. To provide a basis for a national community response to crises and issues of general concern.

VI. To provide a vehicle through which each Black community may avail itself of the aid and advice of the most experienced, skilled, and committed resource persons.

The group was very proactive in achieving its mission and goals. For instance, Dorothy Wills, who was the executive secretary at the time, recalls that while the organization was just starting out, they had a problem regarding the burial of a three-month-old Black baby. At the time, cemeteries in Nova Scotia were segregated, and the government refused to bury this child. Dr. McCurdy called Dr. Wills and instructed her to "send out telegrams to all member organizations and let them we know we're launching a formal protest against the segregated cemeteries in Nova Scotia." The NBCC protested these despicable laws from coast to coast.

One of Dr. Wills' favourite memories is that after a week of demonstrations, the premier of Nova Scotia sent her a telegram saying, "I have given myself sufficient provincial authority to delete this and any such existing legislation from the statute books of Nova Scotia." They won the battle, the baby was buried, and the cemeteries in Nova Scotia became desegregated.

Another prime example of the NBCC achieving its goals was when the federal government acknowledged the group as representing Black people across Canada. Dr. Wills recounts that when the second World Black and African Festival of Arts and Culture in Lagos, Nigeria, sent an invitation to Canada to send a representative, the federal government asked the NBCC to organize the presence of Black people from Canada at the festival. Canada sent about fifty delegates, funded by the government.

In its fifteen years, the NBCC maintained the momentum of Black power and liberation throughout Canada. In 1979, they called for the suspension of the police officer who shot Albert Johnson in his home in Toronto, and they even testified before the Joint House-Senate Committee on the constitution regarding their bill of rights. They also brought attention to the lack of representation of Blacks on television and advertisements, as well as the lack of employment opportunities for Blacks in the media.

The organization dissolved in 1984 due to a lack of funding and internal divisions. As we have seen throughout this chapter, Black organizations in Montreal do not die, they only evolve and multiply; this was true for the NBCC as well, as it went on to become La Ligue des Noirs (Black Coalition of Quebec).

When the Coalition dissolved, Eric Mansfield was the vice president; he and Dan Philip kept the coalition going and got French-speaking immigrants to join. They had many bilingual meetings and became recognized as La Ligue des Noirs in 1984.

Conclusion

When you think of Black power and political activism, Montreal should now be the first city that comes to mind. "They Came, They Saw, and Wanted Change" looked at the various English-speaking West Indian associations that emerged throughout the sixties, such as the Jamaica Association, Trinidad and Tobago Association, Saint Vincent and Grenadines Association, and the Guyana Cultural Association of Montreal.

It illustrated how struggles with covert and overt racism fuelled their creation and represent early Black activism that has positively impacted Black Montrealers. It's important to note that the associations currently face challenges with youth involvement and identification. Many view these not as activist but as party organizations. While the core idea for establishing the organizations in the sixties was to socialize and create a sense of belonging, it's essential to recognize their contributions to Montreal in terms of activism and promoting West Indian culture and integration.

The second half of the chapter looked at the second half of the sixties, when Montreal became the city of Black power conferences that evolved from the Caribbean Conference Committee, such as the Conference on West Indian Affairs and the Congress of Black Writers. This shift from being West Indian-centric to being in the same fight with native-born Black people speaks volumes about Canadian Black identity today. Blacks fostered these groups as a means of survival. Prominent associations such as the Quebec Board of Black Educators still exist.

This chapter has taken you on the journey of Black Montreal in the sixties, from the ninth floor of Sir George Williams University to conferences happening coast to coast with the National Black Coalition of Canada. In the words of Pamela Richmond, "if you look at our history, we're here, despite what happens, we're here. So, we have it in us to progress. So, we need to stand firm."

Chapter 7

A Change in Demography

Yoanna Joseph

The 1960s paved the way for the social movements that ensued, with the emergence of the civil rights and women's liberation movements. However, with change came chaos. The decade was defined by a series of high-profile assassinations which included the deaths of President John F. Kennedy, Attorney General Robert Kennedy, and civil rights activists Martin Luther King and Malcolm X.

Quebec followed suit. The October Crisis was a chain of events that took place in Quebec in the fall of 1970. This crisis was the culmination of a long series of terrorist attacks perpetrated by the Front de libération du Québec (FLQ), a militant movement of French-speaking Quebecers. Raymond Villeneuve, Gabriel Hudon, and Georges Schoeters—the three major leaders of the FLQ—made it their mission to fight for the independence of Quebec. They wanted to liberate themselves from English rule, including the dominance of English culture and language in the majority-French-speaking Quebec.

At this time, Quebec was experiencing vast social, political, and cultural changes, most notably, rising tensions between English- and French-speaking residents.

This civil unrest was joined by the new wave of Black migration that washed over the province. The changes these new residents initiated altered Montreal's history for the better.

Division by Language—Setting the Tone

Between 1963 and 1970, the *Felquistes* were responsible for dozens of robberies and more than two hundred bombings around the city that took the lives of six people. Their actions culminated in the kidnapping of British Trade Commissioner James Cross, and the kidnapping and subsequent murder of Quebec cabinet minister Pierre Laporte in October 1970.

Prime Minister Pierre Trudeau deployed the Armed Forces and invoked the War Measures Act. It was the only time in Canadian history that it had been applied during peacetime. The War Measures Act was in place in October and November before being replaced by the Temporary Measures Act, which lasted until April 1970. These measures allowed the government to suspend civil liberties and arrest citizens without charge. In Quebec, discrimination would sometimes exist based on language and race language and of race.

Civil Uprising and the Emergence of Black Institutions

In the mid-1960s, the Negro Community Centre began to feel the harmful effects of urban renewal. The city had new plans for the city, which caused massive relocation of the population of Saint-Antoine that lost their home. The NCC was a direct victim of this urban renewal, and it caused the disappearance of a lot of its population, and vacant lots remained undeveloped for years. The number of Blacks who could return to Little Burgundy dwindled, as they were now comfortably settled elsewhere. The loss of Black residents and the lack of consistent organizational capacity led to a scattering of the community.

Many local links were broken. In the 1970s, the NCC tried to address this dispersion by opening storefront offices in the neighbourhoods of Côte-des-Neiges, Lasalle, and Notre-Dame-de-Grâce (NDG). These satellite locations were coordinated through the Black Community Central Administration of Quebec (BCCAQ), headquartered in the NCC. The BCCAQ became the umbrella organization for a host of other initiatives such as the Black Youth Television Workshop, the Walker Credit Union, and the Quebec Board of Black Educators.

The Sir George Williams crisis started because of accusations of discrimination and racism concerning a teacher who had falsified the work of West Indian students. The affair led to multiple days of protest by the students and gained international news coverage. In a 1971 *McGill Free Press* article, Tim Hector denounced the priority given to the damaged computers over the students' lives. Hector also recognized the affair as a declaration of Black presence in Montreal society. Although many English-speaking students refused to support the protests after the damage was caused, the activists began to receive support from some French-speaking groups. The Confédération des syndicats nationaux (CSN), Montreal's second-largest labour union, criticized the media for focusing on the material losses of the occupation instead of the racial issues in Canada. French-speaking intellectuals had previously neglected the Black community in Montreal, but the events of the occupation changed their views on racial discrimination in the city.

While this was happening, there was a movement on the global stage to fight for peace and equality. Notably, the US civil rights movement emerged to combat ongoing discrimination. Martin Luther King Jr. encouraged US President Lyndon B. Johnson to sign the Civil Rights Act of 1964. The Immigration Act followed in 1965. This act opened immigration to several more countries, specifically those whose populations were predominantly composed of racialized people. In 1967, the United Nations created the Refugee Protocol and in the same year Canada saw the emergence of immigration regulations introduced in the hopes of precluding discrimination against immigrants.

With the advent of these regulations, throughout the decade, a change in the demography of Quebec became noticeable. The liberation movements of Black Americans and those of Black Canadians appeared to be intrinsically linked as the seventies became a decade of progress in the fight for equality for people of colour. Throughout this decade, inspired by ongoing civil rights movements, Canada saw the emergence of community associations, corporations, and coalitions founded to fight against Black oppression.

Black Immigration to Canada

The makeup of Montreal's Black population had begun to change due to the large spike in Black immigration. The French-speaking Black community grew significantly during this time, as Quebec received an influx of immigrants. This change in demographics led to a phenomenon in which newly settled migrants adopted pluralistic identities. This occurred as Montreal's Black immigrants came to realize that they must band together to fight the racism and discrimination they faced. It was increasingly clear that it was important to unify the Black population and invest in the development of Black communities. There was a lack of infrastructure to meet the needs of the growing Black population, and there was also a lack of support for the development of Black identity and Black culture as a whole. Throughout the immigration boom, organizations emerged to address these needs.

The National Black Coalition of Canada

The injustice faced by the Black community in the Sir George Williams Affair sent significant shock waves across the country. It reaffirmed the importance of having a national collective designed to fight racism and discrimination in Canada. This event helped to create one of the major organizations dedicated to uniting Black communities in Canada, the National Black Coalition of Canada (NBCC), founded on October 19th, 1969, shortly after the Sir George Williams crisis. The NBCC's head office was situated at 8130 Place Vaujours in Anjou. The organization's founding members were Dr. Clarence Bayne, Dr. Dorothy Wills, and E.D. Clarke.

Prior to that, there was no central organization that succeeded in forming a national coalition for the advancement of the Black community in Canada. The organization's motto was "Identity, Unity, and Liberation," and its goal was to solidify the Black cause and fight anti-Black racism on a national level. The two central points of the NBCC's constitution were "to ensure that the unique cultural heritage and contributions of black people of Canada become a functional part of the emerging [Canadian mosaic]" and "to foster through the black experience and culture a spirit of racial pride, identity and community." The NBCC also encouraged Black Canadian political representation. It was the first Canadian national civil rights organization, assembling twenty-eight Black organizations from across Canada under its insignia.

The Coalition took inspiration from the National Association for the Advancement of Colored People (NAACP) in the United States and its two branches in Canada, which were led by Gus Wedderburn in Nova Scotia, and Irene Duncun in British Columbia. This coalition emerged as Black Canadians were faced with new challenge of a growing population fueled by immigration and a mounting birth rate.

In October of 1972, the NBCC started its newsletter titled *Habari Kijiji*, which translates to *Village News*. The newsletter was regularly circulated to NBCC members. *Habari Kijiji* published articles, such as opinion pieces, written by community members. They also routinely printed creative literary works such as poetry, fiction, and non-fiction texts. In addition, the newsletter kept the public informed of upcoming events and activities, with news about the development of other Black associations in various cities.

The National Black Coalition of Canada established offices across the country, one of which being at 1610 Sherbrooke Street West in Montreal. This local research institute was created under the guidance of Dr. Clarence S. Bayne, chairman of the NBCC. These research centres collected everything pertinent to the Black community, including videos, bibliographies, interviews, photographs, projection slides, and more. The purpose of the centre was to conduct research of interest to the Black community and to allow Black Canadians to conduct their own fact-finding. Most notably, the NBCC Research Institute conducted a study of the Sir George Williams Affair, and later, of African-language studies in Canada. Furthermore, they provided a library, public information services, and educational services to promote continued research. The NBCC also offered instructional courses, seminars, and lecture discussions, a psycho-educational program, job counselling, and economic advisory services. All these programs were created so that the Black community could have a place where they could be empowered, find healing, and thrive.

For instance, Black Canadians were often subjected to employment discrimination. The job counselling service was designed to target this issue. The psycho-educational program was put in place in hopes of countering the negativity children faced in school. The goal was to encourage pride and self-acceptance and address the effects of discrimination and bias that Black children experienced.

In summary, the programs from the research institute were designed to support the community in varying ways. The NBCC had difficulty sustaining memberships, however. They also encountered problems with association chapters. In 1984, the organization collapsed due to internal strife and funding issues.

The Black Theatre Workshop

The Black Theatre Workshop (BTW) was established to encourage Black art and culture. With the Black population growing in Montreal, new immigrants and residents were in search of a place for the creation of Black art and theatrical expression. A forerunner to the Black Theatre Workshop was the Trinidad and Tobago group. This group promoted the works of West Indian playwrights. From 1965 to 1970, they were under the direction of Johnny Caits. In 1968, there was a shift from a focus on West Indian identities to those of the Black community as a whole.

The Trinidad and Tobago group created their own Drama Committee. They wanted to create an organization in the image of their city, its vibrancy, and its culture. They looked to establish a place where they could develop Black playwrights and performers, showcase Black art that would include the perspectives of all related ethnic backgrounds, employing Black youth, Black directors, and Black playwrights. Although it was not the first Black theatre to emerge in Canada, the Black Theatre Workshop is the oldest running Black theatre, created in 1972. Dr. Clarence Bayne acted as the president and the organization's first artistic director. He was also the founder of the initial Trinidad Drama Committee. Other members of BTW were Vice-President Ken Pilgrim, Secretary Jacinta Thomas, Treasurer Violet Bolton, director and playwright David Edgecombe, and dance instructor and designer Walter Elliot.

The Black Theatre Workshop conducted its first series of playwright and actor workshops in 1973, and in 1974, they had their first two major productions.

Throughout the 1970s, BTW held its productions at the Negro Community Centre (1974), the Revue Theatre (1974–77), Moyse Hall at McGill University, the Centaur Theater, and the NDG Black Community Centre. In the years that followed, the BTW became the artistic company we know today.

Caribbean Immigration and Maison d'Haïti

The French-speaking Caribbean community also expanded during the 1970s. To this day, the Haitian community contributes the most Black, afro-descendent immigrants to Quebec, with its population growing dramatically throughout the decade. The first large wave of Haitian immigrants arrived in Canada between 1967 and 1972. This first wave was called the "Brain Drain," as it consisted essentially of Haitian intellectuals who fled the Duvalier dictatorship.

Although the Duvalier dictatorship continued, the second wave of Haitian immigrants who arrived between 1973 and 1994 no longer only comprised Haitian intellectuals, but also the middle and other classes from Haiti. These newcomers met the labour needs of Quebec factories.

This massive influx of Haitian immigrants inspired the creation of Maison d'Haïti. This organization assisted Haitian immigrants with their integration into Quebec. It was founded by young Haitians who felt the need to have a specific place where new immigrants could receive support. They also wanted a place where the women of the community could meet, exchange ideas, and bring Haitian culture to life in Montreal. Since its formation, it has addressed several issues encountered by the Haitian community, primarily francization and access to employment. The organization also helped illiterate newcomers learn how to read and write.

Maison d'Haïti has had its headquarters in several locations across the city. However, since 2016, the organization has been located in Villeray-Saint-Michel, home to a large Haitian population. In addition to the integration assistance it offers newcomers, Maison d'Haïti invests in young people by offering them several activities. It also avidly supports Black artists through their participation in the Afro-Urban Festival and *Pakapala TV*. The organization is a pillar of the French-speaking Black immigrant community of Montreal, but more importantly, the Maison d'Haïti supports all immigrant communities in Saint Michel, as it offers multiple activities for immigrants and their families.

The Black Studies Center (BSC)

Another community organization that gathered information from the Black community in Montreal is the Black Studies Center (BSC). This Côte-des-Neiges centre was designed as a place where Black residents could conduct community research while accessing support and resources.

The BSC was incorporated in 1972. It was located at 1968 de Maisonneuve Boulevard in Montreal West and was part of the Black Community Central Administration of Quebec, later renamed the Black Community Council of Quebec. The library had over four thousand international documents on Black people and Black culture, which the council made available to its members. Dr. Clarence Bayne also conducted research and surveys with the Special Research Department analyzing the growth and development of the Black community. Bayne acquired a property in 1973 which became the permanent home of the Black Studies Center.

The Black Studies Center published its first monthly bulletin in June 1974, called *The Black Studies Center Newsletter*. The newsletter was designed to strengthen community ties between members and other organizations, and to inform readers about upcoming events. The BSC also sponsored workshops, seminars, lectures, and other cultural activities.

The Negro Community Centre

The Negro Community Centre (NCC) of Montreal was the hub of the Black community. The NCC had to expand its geographical reach as a large part of the population relocated to different neighbourhoods due to the urban renewal of Little Burgundy.

Starting in the 1960s, the city succeeded in acquiring 75 percent of the land in Little Burgundy. This had dire effects on the Black community. By the time the city constructed social housing, most of the community had moved due to the destruction and gentrification of the area. Due to this mass relocation, the Negro Community Centre had to open offices in other areas of Montreal. The office in Little Burgundy remained active, as did branches in Lasalle, NDG, and Côte-des-Neiges.

The centre has provided services for over fifty thousand community members. The most used service was their daycare program. They also offered other services, such as a program for community elders, adult French classes, fitness classes, individual counseling, personal assistance (for new immigrants, unemployed people, and children struggling academically) and more. In 1982, 680 people benefited from their programs and services. In 1983, they also implemented a legal aid program.

Much like the National Black Coalition of Canada, the Negro Community Centre also published a monthly newspaper, *AfroCan*, that detailed all upcoming activities and events. The NCC was part of a larger organization called the Black Community Council of Quebec (BCCQ), which was the predominant Black organization in NDG from 1970 to 1995. It was the voice of the Black community, responsible for ensuring the economic, psychological, and political well-being of Blacks in NDG. They openly spoke on Black issues in Canada, as well as on issues specifically targeting English-speaking members of the community. The NCC filed for bankruptcy in 2014, although it had ceased all activity in 1993. In November of 2014, their building was demolished. To this day, there are still groups trying to restore the Negro Community Centre as it proved to be one of the most essential Black organizations in Montreal. The project to bring back the NCC has been approved, and the Negro Community Center will, in the future, be renamed the Centre for Canadians of African Descent.

Carifiesta and Caribbean Culture in Montreal

Carifiesta, also called "Jump-Up" or "Carnival," has been an annual celebration in Montreal since the 1970s. In 1974, Montreal held its first edition, which comes back annually, held every second weekend of July. This event is organized by the Caribbean Cultural Festivities Association, formerly known as the Caribbean Cultural Initiative.

During the first years of the festivities, the Quebec Black Community Development Project was in charge and oversaw activities. They created the Carifiesta Committee that later took over. They also created a "Black Week" where musicians, singers, and dancers from all over Montreal gathered to celebrate Black Caribbean and Canadian culture. The committee famously hosted a parade within the same week, every year.

Carifiesta is one of Montreal's most colourful and exciting parades. The community celebrates with costumes, music, and much more. The French and English Islands all have their parade floats, and they coordinate the whole event together. In recent years, other Caribbean events have taken place at around the same time as Carifiesta, for instance the Jamaica Day festival. Carifiesta honours Montreal's Caribbean community and its history. The celebration pays homage to its African, Caribbean, and Christian heritages.

Carifiesta allows us to acknowledge and appreciate the diverse Caribbean cultures that contribute to a multicultural Montreal, as well as educating and sensitizing the next generation of Caribbean people as well as the rest of the Quebec population.

Big Brothers, Big Sisters

The Big Brothers, Big Sisters organization supported Black youth year-round. This organization evolved over the years from several different efforts designed to help at-risk boys and girls. In 1904, Ernest K. Coulter of New York City recognized that an increasing number of boys were experiencing legal difficulties. In 1905, a Mrs. John O'Keefe, after learning of the Big Brothers program's success, began a Big Sisters program, also in the US.

Nine years later, with the need for an innovative solution to the growing delinquency rate, Big Brothers began operation in Canada. In December 1972, Big Brothers Canada separated from the American organization and became a self-governing group. Within four years, Big Brothers Canada grew to include 110 agencies across Canada, supporting eight thousand boys. Two years later, in 1976, the office in Montreal opened and by the end of the following year, four agencies were established in the province, with locations in Montreal, the West Island, Victoriaville, and Quebec City.

Much has changed over the years, including the move to bring together Big Brothers and Big Sisters under one agency. They also expanded their programs to meet the changing needs of families and young people. It was their mission to empower the youth through mentorship. To address the need for diversity, the company implemented several programs with mentors from diverse backgrounds, such as the "Black'n Role" mentoring program, which allows children to seek guidance from Black mentors. This program helps create a positive sense of identity in Black children, pairing a Black child and a mentor from the same community, who acts as a positive role model. The purpose of the program is to help young mentees improve their social and personal skills while focusing on academic success and involvement within the community. Since its implementation, the organization has helped over a hundred children.

Chapter 8

Growth and Innovation: Building a Black Cultural Mosaic in 1980s–1990s Montreal

Donna Fabiola Ingabire

Visible minorities have a long history in Canada. The adoption of the immigration points system in 1967, which saw the Canadian government prioritize language ability, education levels, and skills rather than nationality and race was a huge step away from past discriminatory immigration policies. At the request of Robert Andras, who was the minister of Manpower and Immigration, immigration policy went through a significant evaluation in 1973. Proposals made during this process led to major discussions and the eventual creation of a special immigration committee. The committee's main objective was to hold public hearings about immigration all over the country, and examine the proposals made during the evaluation. This special committee made sixty-five recommendations, and most of them were accepted by the Liberal government and included in the Immigration Act of 1976.

The Immigration Act marked an important chapter in the history of Canadian immigration policies. Whereas previous policies had restricted the number of non-white and Jewish immigrants allowed into Canada, the act promoted diversity and non-discrimination in immigrant selection processes. The act, eventually implemented in 1978, led to a significant change in the origins and racial makeup of Canadian immigrants. As a result of this reform, a significant number of Africans, Haitians, and Latin Americans immigrated to Montreal in the 1970s and onwards. While some of these immigrants were fleeing political upheavals in sub-Saharan African countries in the early 1990s, others also moved to the city to further their studies or find employment. They also came from both French- and English-speaking countries. French-speaking African immigrants came from Zaire (now Democratic Republic of the Congo), Côte d'Ivoire, Cameroon, Burundi, Rwanda, and Congo; whereas English-speaking African immigrants came from Egypt, South Africa, Tanzania, Kenya, Ghana, and Nigeria. Despite their fluency in French and English, and the fact that they were university-educated, these new Black Montrealers had a hard time attaining employment. Changes in Canadian immigration policies had not necessarily meant a changed attitude towards Black Canadians in Montreal, and thus new immigrants to the city faced the same challenges that plagued earlier Black immigrants. They too endured racism and discrimination.

This chapter's main objective is to explore how Black Montrealers—both newly immigrated and those who had been here for generations—responded to these challenges through community-building approaches that ensured their survival in the period ranging from 1980 to 2000.

Montreal International Jazz Festival

Though jazz has a long history in Montreal, by the 1960s rock'n'roll had taken over and replaced it in popularity. In 1975, Rouè-Doudou Boicel, a young Guyanese immigrant who had moved to Quebec in 1970, decided to revitalize the genre in which many had lost interest. Set on changing the narrative around jazz and promoting Black culture in Montreal, Boicel established the Rising Sun Celebrity Jazz Club. The venue coined its infamous slogan, "Jazz is not dead," opened its doors, and hosted an array of Canadian and American musicians as well as local talent. The club also attracted international Black artists who wanted to support the only Black jazz club owner in the city. In 1978, Boicel attended a jazz festival in Vermont to see Rahsaan Kirk perform, and it inspired him to start something similar in Montreal. Boicel successfully convinced a man in charge of renting out Place des Arts halls to rent him a place to host the event. The festival, called the Rising Sun Festijazz, attracted an impressive lineup of international jazz artists such as Dexter Gordon and Sarah Vaughan. It was also at this festival that both B. B. King and Oscar Peterson got a chance to play for a large audience for the first time in Montreal. The festival successfully ran for three years at Place des Arts. It inspired countless other major jazz festivals around the world, and even international artists such as Taj Mahal, Nina Simone, Muddy Waters, and Ray Charles graced Montreal stages at Boicel's invitation.

In 1980, two years after the Rising Sun Festijazz's inauguration, Québécois businesspeople and jazz enthusiasts Alain Simard, André Menard, Alain de

Grosbois, and Denyse McCann founded the Montreal International Jazz Festival. The first edition of the festival was held on Saint Helen's Island, at the same location where the Montreal Expo was held fourteen years earlier. It was attended by some twelve thousand concertgoers and attracted a hundred artists from July 2nd–10th of that year. Performers at the festival included Ray Charles, Vic Vogel, Gary Burton, and Chick Corea. In 1986, the festival hosted over a thousand artists and had become a free outdoor event open to everyone. It moved to Place des Arts in 1988, adjacent to Boicel's Rising Sun club. With two million people in attendance at its twenty-fifth edition in 2004, the festival placed first in the *Guinness Book of World Records* for the largest jazz festival in the world. Moreover, for jazz enthusiasts, the Montreal Jazz Festival is classed as one of the best in the world, with artists coming from Africa, Central and South America, Canada, Europe and the US to perform. The diverse body of musical genres performed at the festival includes Reggae, Cajun, Pop, Blues, Rock, Latin, and more.

The Montreal International Jazz Festival has not been without controversy. In 2018, one of its performances had to be cancelled because its production, *SLAV*, involved a mostly white cast performing Black American slave spirituals. For many Black Montreal performers, particularly those whose ancestors experienced slavery, the performance was a slap in the face. It was reminiscent of the discrimination they are made to endure within the performance industry. It also further highlighted the ongoing issue of white people taking up Black spaces and jobs that might more appropriately have gone to Black candidates.

The International Jazz Festival has been an extremely important and successful part of Montreal's history, with artists coming from all over the world to participate. It is important to remember that a Black immigrant man from Guyana not only revived jazz when many believed the genre was dead, but also organized the first *ever* successful jazz festival in the city. During the mid-1970s and '80s, when many jazz clubs had disappeared from Montreal, the Rising Sun became the only club hosting a high calibre of international jazz artists. Despite the arrival of the Montreal International Jazz Festival leading to declining interest in the Rising Sun Festijazz, in his interview with Alain Brunet, Rouè-Doudou Boicel said that he was not bitter. What troubled him was the fact that public institutions and the media chose to forget that it was his efforts that brought jazz back to Montreal.

In recent years, Rouè Boicel has received numerous accolades for his cultural and social contributions to Montreal and Quebec as a whole.

The West Island Black Community Association

The West Island Black Community Association (WIBCA) is one of a network of Black community associations that evolved out of the NCC's outreach programs. These programs had several purposes: (1) expanding the reach of the NCC to provide Black representation for the wider Black community, (2) providing a unified voice for the community, and (3) bringing the diverse and fragmented Black community under a concept of Pan-Africanism.

The outreach programs of the NCC were introduced by Carl Whittaker and have resulted in the growth of the Black community in the sixties and seventies, the settlement of new Black immigrants, as well as the movement of Canadian-born Black populations from Little Burgundy and Central Montreal to new developments in LaSalle, Côte-des-Neiges, Notre-Dame-de-Grâce, the West Island, the South Shore, Pierrefonds, and Montreal North. This movement of populations out of the Little Burgundy and downtown areas brought Black community members under different regional jurisdictions. Such demographic change and "donut redistribution" of the population had a major impact on the structure of the Negro Community Centre and its original mandate to provide services in a limited geographic area.

Studies of human social systems show that the greater the fragmentation, the less objective and subjective wellbeing are enjoyed by the members of the group in question. In the seventies and eighties, the leaders of the new Black immigrant groups in Montreal recognized this problem and moved aggressively to create alliances and coalitions. It is from these coalitions that the WIBCA was born.

In 1982, upon realizing the lack of organized and diversified activities for their youth and children, two Black mothers, Norma Husbands and Margaret Jolly, decided to create an organization. Though at this point it was not formal and there was no membership, a youth worker named Momoh Kokulatomba, from the Black

Community Council of Quebec, agreed to work for them. The YMCA then provided the organization with space and an animator named Carl Whittaker. The two women also contacted Gerald "Gerry" Weiner, who was the mayor of Dollard-des-Ormeaux. At a Black Professionals meeting with the mayor, it was determined that the West Island needed a Black association.

In the spring of 1982, WIBCA started organizing activities for the youth within the community. Trips were organized by Kokulatomba, and basketball and karate lessons were offered at the Lakeside Heights school gym. On June 7th, 1982, with the support of volunteers, the WIBCA was able to hold its very first public meeting. A steering committee was created to help the organization decide on their strategy and structure. During their second public meeting in 1982, the community decided to name their new organization the West Island Black Community Association. At that time, three internal committees were created: the education committee, the social/membership committee, and the constitution committee. WIBCA created its charter in 1983 and registered with the province as a Non-Profit Organization.

WIBCA events such as the banquet and holiday parties, which became annual events, were organized that year. After continued growth in 1984, the organization was able to move from holding meetings in members' homes to an official address at 11072 Gouin Boulevard. Various youth groups also emerged within WIBCA, with their primary focus being to organize community activities with the guidance of the older youth.

By its five-year anniversary in 1987, WIBCA had become a significant part of the West Island community and was chaired by Donald MacFarlane, Norma Husbands, Marie Garnett, and Winston Brathwaite. During this period, the organization was running several collaborative projects thanks to strategic relationship building. In addition to courses on Black history at John Rennie High School, a Saturday morning tutoring program was also provided to the youth of the community. This program, led both by WIBCA and the Quebec Board of Black Educators, was provided at Riverdale High School and Herbert Purcell Elementary School. It was also during this period that the WIBCA created a Community Outreach with the law enforcement officers of Station Eleven and Station Twelve, with the main objective being crime prevention. This important alliance resulted in WIBCA representatives playing the role of mediator between the law and Black youth.

The organization continues to hold local governments and law enforcement accountable for the racism and police brutality that Black people, especially young people, face in Montreal. In June 2020, following the death of George Floyd, the association held a town hall where mayors present were made aware of the disappointment felt by members of the West Island Black community at the failure of all elected officials in the city to make a statement denouncing anti-Black racism and police brutality. The organization's efforts resulted in Mayors John Belvedere of Pointe Claire and Jim Beis of Pierrefonds-Roxboro promising to make statements in the coming days. Jim Beis made his statement the following morning and acknowledged that systemic racism exists. Mayor Beis also stated that he had communicated with other mayors of the West

Island and requested a meeting where they could discuss how to combat racism in the city.

Over the years, WIBCA has continued to build strategic relationships with other organizations, communities, and government departments. This has allowed them to continue their mission of advocating for and providing services to community members. For example, in the early to mid-1990s with Reynold Clarke and Eileen White as chairs, the organization formed partnerships with Emploi Quebec, Batshaw Youth and Family Services, YMCA, le Centre d'intégration Multiservices de l'Ouest-de-l'Île, Human Resources Canada, the Quebec Ministry of Citizenship and Immigration, Maison des Jeunes A-MA-Baie, the Montreal Urban Community police stations in the West Island, and the Cloverdale Multi-Resources of Pierrefonds.

By its 20th anniversary in 2002, the organization had managed to build more important relationships with politicians on the federal, provincial, and municipal levels as well as with the Lester B. Pearson School Board.

It was also at the celebration of their 20th anniversary that the organization decided to adopt the theme "Perseverance—a Fundamental Requirement for Success." The following year, WIBCA's focus was on "rebuilding, expansion and consolidation." This was extremely important for WIBCA. The Montreal radio station CJAD had just aired a dialogue entitled "Community in Crisis," the main premise of which was the significant number of young men in the community dying prematurely. After the radio discussion, in which the WIBCA had partaken, the organization's members reflected on how they could help prevent youth delinquency and antisocial behaviour. WIBCA was able to offer new programs and services with the main objective of offering better protection and safety measures for the community.

For example, through their partnerships with groups that deliver community services in Montreal and the Côte-des-Neiges Black Community Association, the WIBCA was able to establish what is known today as the African Canadian Development and Prevention Network (ACDPN), a network of organizations providing effective and accessible services to the Black community and strengthening Black families.

The WIBCA was able to obtain government grants to support community crime prevention, thanks to the support of Leith Hamilton, Michael Gittens, and other community organizations, that allowed it to be a true representative of the people it serves. This program's main goal was to decrease the gap between senior and youth members of the community. Thanks to the grants and efforts by Tiffany Callender—the current chief executive officer of the Federation of African Canadian Economics—and Melissa Alleyne, the WIBCA was able to start another project titled D.R.E.A.M. (Delivering Real Empowerment and Motivation) Drop-In Centre to support the youth.

The WIBCA also received a donation of $6,000 from Errol Johnson. Mr. Johnson had raised the funds through the West Island Blues Festival, which he organized. Ever since then, this festival has become an important part of the West Island community and is held yearly during the summer to raise funds for local charities. Mr. Johnson continues to play an important role in the WIBCA and in 2005 he and Margaret Jolly helped them obtain Registered Charity status under the Income Tax Act.

From 1997 to 2002, the organization was chaired by Kenneth Bynoe. He was later joined by Veronica Johnson, and they chaired the organization together from 2002 to 2007. From 2007 to 2017 the organization was led by Tomacuita James, Akwasi Yeboah, Elizabeth-Ann Williams, and Kemba Mitchell. With the Skills Link Grant provided by the Canadian government's Youth Employment Strategy, the WIBCA was able to support young people from marginalized communities. The funding also allowed them to start a meal program for Black families at Springdale School as well as an after-school tutoring program.

The Covid 19 pandemic proved challenging for the organization. Due to Covid measures that included social distancing, the organization was limited in its fundraising activities. They also had to halt all programs usually held in person. To overcome this challenge, they moved their activities online and were able to create new programs. Among them was Black Girls Gather: a Book Club. The book club was founded by Mariame Touré and Fabiola Ngamaleu Teumeni in 2020. In addition to the founders, the club is also run by Vanessa Manroop, Joanna Kanga, Miss Thaisha, Miss Khadija, Miss Alivia, and Amélia Souffrant. Touré and Manroop were part of the WIBCA's youth program and continue volunteering in other programs offered by the organization.

WIBCA also started other virtual programs such as the Senior Fit program and Senior Surf. The lifting of pandemic restrictions has made it possible for them to create the free mentored Robotics Club for youth aged nine to nineteen, to encourage teens to venture into science, technology, engineering, and mathematics. Moreover, the WIBCA started a scholarship program in collaboration with author Alvina Ryan. Through this program, the organization offers three higher education scholarships to youth, and another one called the Empowered Woman Scholarship, offered to a female student from the West Island.

The WIBCA has faced many challenges over the years that have been overcome through effective community organizing. For example, in the early 1990s, the organization faced an expropriation crisis after the Quebec Ministry of Transport bought the shopping centre where the organization's office was located. This forced them to stop all programs and go back to holding meetings in members' basements. Mrs. Eileen White, one of the founding members of the organization, took charge of a Building Fund. It was through this fund, with the support of members and MNA Russell Williams, that the WIBCA was finally able to raise enough money for a mortgage for the building at 48A-D 4th Avenue South, Roxboro. Mrs. White also ensured that the organization got funding from the bank by putting up her own house as guarantee. In 2019, the organization finally finished paying off their mortgage and amassed over $100,000 for its renovation.

Poster of Town Hall Meeting held by WIBCA on June 7th, 2020 after the murder of George Floyd. Artwork by Amélia Souffrant.

The Council for Black Aging Community of Montreal

(bacm.org, 2022)

Photographer, Name of photograph, photograph, CBACM, 2022, https://cbacm.org.

The Council for Black Aging Community of Montreal Inc. (CBACM) is a charitable, non-profit organization created in 1987. It was established after several community members realized that the needs of English-speaking seniors in the Black community were being ignored by community service centres and traditional health care institutions in Montreal. Upon further study of the issue, they concluded that Black seniors' health needs were deliberately ignored due to historical and systemic discrimination faced by Black people in Montreal and Canada as a whole. Therefore, community members took it upon themselves to change the system and how it treated Black seniors. The main objectives of their work were to illustrate how the Black community had made important contributions to Canadian society, and to advocate on behalf of seniors. They also wanted to demonstrate to all levels of government the urgency of the need for a change in the treatment of Black people, especially seniors.

They argued that Canadians of African and West Indian/Caribbean descent had been mistreated and made unwelcome through various discriminatory policies, despite having always been honourable and loyal citizens. They believed that since section fifteen of the Canadian Charter of Rights and Freedoms makes it clear that "every individual is equal before and under the law and has the right to equal protection and equal benefit of the law without discrimination and, in particular, without discrimination based on race, national or ethnic origin, colour, religion, sex, age or mental or physical disability," then Black Canadians, particularly senior members of the community, deserved non-discriminatory treatment. The founders also wanted to help seniors understand how legislation implemented by all levels of the government affects them specifically. Alongisde all this, the CBACM also conducts research to address the needs of Black elders.

Since its inception in 1987, the organization's main objective has been delivering services to Black seniors, providing them with a network of emotional support, and facilitating their participation in cultural, social, recreational, and educational activities. The organization is also committed to ensuring that Black seniors have an improved quality of life and enhanced autonomy in their homes.

The CBACM organizes its activities in three sections, namely education, exercise/fitness, and social/recreational. To combat the isolation that many seniors face, social and recreational activities are organized for them. The activities allow seniors to make friends and create community while enriching their knowledge and health. Some of the exercise and fitness activities are aqua fit, chair yoga, choir, and folk cultural dance. Educational development activities include computer, nutrition, painting and art, and arts and crafts classes. For the future, the CBACM hopes to own a residence to serve the specific needs of Montreal's Black elders. The organization also wishes to procure and own their own premises for the council.

Club Balattou and Nuits d'Afrique

Prior to immigration reforms in the 1960s and 1970s, Canada's discriminatory immigration policies made it extremely difficult for immigrants from non-white countries to move to Canada. The 1911 Order-in-Council whose aim was to ban the entry of Black Americans who were fleeing American white supremacist violence is an example. This bill, approved by Prime Minister Sir Wilfrid Laurier, stated that, "for a period of one year from and after the date hereof the landing in Canada shall be and the same is prohibited of any immigrants belonging to the Negro race, which race is deemed unsuitable to the climate and requirements of Canada."

During this time, to halt Black immigration, Canadian authorities engaged in tactics that made immigration extremely challenging for Blacks looking for safety in Canada. These ranged from subjecting Black people to difficult medical examinations at the border to making immigration documents inaccessible to them. As a result of these racist immigration policies, fewer than 1 percent of immigrants allowed into Canada were of African descent from 1897 to 1930.

Throughout the early 20th century, Blacks were often allowed to immigrate to Canada only as domestic workers, railroad workers, or as international students from the Caribbean, though that was less common.

However, by the 1960s, Europe was no longer capable of providing Canada with enough immigrants to satisfy its growing economic needs, and racist immigration selection processes were being challenged by organizations such as the Negro Citizenship Association and the Canadian Jewish Congress. The Canadian government moved toward a less racist immigration policy reflective of its time.

The new policy introduced on October 1st, 1967, used a point system to select immigrants instead of the previous ethnic and race criteria. Through this system, immigrants were selected based on their French or English language skills, their education level, and their labour skills. The point system allowed for a great diversification of Canada and by 1977, 50 percent of immigrants who came to the country came from regions that had previously been heavily restricted, such as Africa, Latin America, the Caribbean, and Asia.

These changes in immigration policy had a significant impact on the number of Africans in Canada. For example, between 1946 and 1950, immigration of Africans to Canada counted for only 0.3 percent. By 1970, that had risen to 2 percent. As a result, African immigrants who settled in Montreal during this time often found themselves alone and with a very small African community. Requirements for Africans wishing to move to Canada remained very strict from the 1970s to the '90s, and only those with extremely high levels of education were allowed to immigrate.

Out of 441,253 immigrants who had moved to Canada from 1975 to 1978, only 27,252 were from African countries. Canada preferred immigrants who were entrepreneurs and could provide jobs to Canadians, or those who came from specific English-speaking countries like Ghana and Nigeria. What this meant, especially for the entrepreneurs, is that most of them belonged to wealthy European and Asian African communities, an example being the sixteen thousand mostly non-Black South Africans who moved to Canada as South Africa was transitioning from apartheid rule to Black leadership between 1973 and 1983, and the seven thousand Ugandan Asians accepted by Canada after Uganda's President Idi Amin expelled them. This trend of the Canadian government accepting mostly Asians applied also for immigrants coming from Tanzania and Kenya.

In addition to these English-speaking immigrants, there were also French-speaking immigrants who settled in Quebec. They came from former French colonies like Cameroon, the Congo, Zaire (now the Democratic Republic of the Congo) and Côte d'Ivoire. They also came from Burundi, Rwanda, Togo, Mali, Gabon, Chad, and Central Africa. Though these immigrants were coming to Quebec for myriad reasons such as love, education, and to search for a better life, it is important to note that many of them were also fleeing their countries due to socio-political conflicts in 1990s Africa, particularly in Mali, Gabon, Chad, Côte d'Ivoire and Central Africa. Others were fleeing military rule, one-party regimes, and the 1994 genocide in Rwanda. Most of these African immigrants who settled in Quebec chose to live in the metropolitan areas of Montreal, Gatineau (Ottawa), and Quebec City.

Like earlier Black immigrants, African immigrants settling in Montreal were highly educated. In a survey conducted in 1983, over 80 percent of Africans in Canada were found to have a university-level education, with 14.3 percent of them having a PhD, 38.4 percent a master's, and over 80 percent a BA. Unfortunately, due to anti-Black racism in Quebec, Africans' high level of education was not reflected in their employment rate. For example, 64 percent of the Africans interviewed in the study stated that they did not have employment in the previous one to five years despite having permission to work.

To ensure their survival and combat the difficulties that come with moving to a foreign country, Africans created cultural events, clubs, and organizations that served their needs. The most popular of these are Nuits d'Afrique and Club Balattou, both established by a young immigrant by the name of Lamine Touré in 1987. Mr. Touré had arrived in Montreal in 1974 for what was supposed to be a one-month stay. A day before his planned departure, he met an old friend who asked him to stay in Montreal. In an interview with Jean-Sébastien Josset of *Jeune Afrique*, Mr. Touré said that though at that time the African community in Montreal was very small, he quickly understood that at some point it would grow. He wanted to create a place where newly-arrived African immigrants could be welcomed.

He started off by creating Café Créole in 1976. Touré shared ownership of the bar with Alex Boicel, the son of legendary jazz club owner Rouè-Doudou Boicel. Together, Boicel and Touré turned the café into a place where Africans could socialize, take a drink, and eat together. In addition to this, newly arrived immigrants could get help there with tasks such as figuring out working papers and permits. For their kindness, Boicel and Touré often received the latest records of music from overseas.

Café Créole closed its doors in the early 1980s, and Touré decided to open a new bar that would also accommodate non-Africans. He called his new bar Club Balattou, a play on the French *bar a tout* meaning "bar for all." Club Balattou became a huge hit, with a clientele from all the city's diverse communities, and Touré was able to hire a dozen employees. For the first time in Montreal, both Quebecers and immigrant communities had a place to go to enjoy African music. The following year, Touré decided to create a festival titled Nuits d'Afrique. Just like Club Balattou, Nuits d'Afrique focused on music by artists from non-Western backgrounds who were infrequently featured in other music festivals.

Club Balattou and Nuits d'Afrique popularized African music in 1980s Montreal and in North America. Prior to this, the genre was enjoyed mostly within African cultural communities. It also helped promote local African artists and their music not just in Montreal, but internationally too.

Today, the Festival International Nuits d'Afrique is considered North America's largest African music festival. It takes place every July for two weeks and artists from Africa, the Caribbean, and Latin America have graced its stage over the years. Among them have been Ivorian artist Tiken Jah Fakoly, Nigerian Femi Kuti, Rwandan-Canadian Corneille, Malian duo Amadou et Mariam, Nigerian King Sunny Adé, Senegalese Youssou N'Dour, Haitian group Tabou Combo, and Guadeloupean group Kassav.

For his contributions to the Montreal and Quebec cultural scenes, Touré has received a number of awards, including the 2013 Ordre national du Québec, the most distinctive honour offered by the Quebec government. He also became a member of the Order of Canada in

2018 for his promotion of African, Caribbean, and Latin American cultures in Montreal.

Creation of the Black Academic Scholarship Fund

Education is an important tool for societal elevation, and it continues to be inaccessible to many marginalized people, particularly Black Canadians. Black learners often feel alienated by an education system that fails to teach them Black and African-Canadian history and culture, or provide them with Black educators. Racist attitudes are pervasive in Canadian education systems; for example, in a study conducted by Professor George Dei of the Ontario Institute for Studies in Education, it was found that many teachers believed that the Ontario education system was not to blame for Black students' high dropout rate. They instead believed that the background of Black students, such as their values and attitudes toward education, as well as academic and social deficiencies in their families, were to blame.

Members of a so-called "educational organization" named the Canadian Association for Free Expression accused the Toronto District School Board of "being punch drunk on minorities." They also believed that Black learners were underachieving because of a "demonstrably lower Negro IQ." These negative sentiments toward Black students, as well as a lack of Black and African Canadian studies within the Canadian public school curriculum, has resulted in a great number of Black students dropping out. This in turn affects the economic status of Black people in Quebec, who despite sometimes having been in the province for many generations, face high unemployment and a disproportionate number of low-income households in comparison to other populations.

It is for all these reasons that the Black Academic Scholarship Fund (BASF) was established in 1981 by a group of Montreal Black businesspersons and professionals who were also members of the Black Community Forum. Founders of the organization were asked by the Forum to provide a detailed report of their activities to address the issues that Black learners and the Black community at large were facing. Members of the BASF provide students with financial support for their studies, hence also improving the economic status of the Black community.

Pictured: President and Founder of the Black Academic Scholarship Fund, Mrs. Sylvia Piggott, 1939–2021.

From the beginning, the BASF has been committed to empowering Black students and helping them accomplish their goals, employing Canadian Black scholar Rosalind Hampton's research on Black learners. Hampton studies the rise of Afrocentric public schools in Canada, especially in Montreal. Though these schools have been met with controversy, their proponents created them because many Black learners continue to be failed and neglected by the Eurocentric Canadian public education system. Hampton also argues that community-based educational programs that take the lived experiences of Black youth into consideration and "provide them with new ways of understanding and responding to the world around them" are more beneficial for their advancement.

Since Black people are not a monolith and come from many different cultural backgrounds (especially in a city like Montreal) the founders needed strategies that would advance their goals of supporting Black learners of many origins throughout the education system. To achieve this, they put aside all negative sentiments, cultural differences, arguments fueled by ideological differences, and stereotypes that separate the Black community.

Pictured: Current board members of the BASF. From left to right: Allison Saunders, secretary, chair Media & Social Media; Garry Saunders, member, chair Mentorship Committee; Sylvia Piggott, deceased founder and former president of the BASF; Kathleen Suite, current president of the BASF; Dr. Kelly Hennegan, past scholarship recipient and member chair, Scholarship & Alumni Committees; and Glen Gunning. Unpictured: Chike Odenigbo, 2017 recipient of the Jackie Robinson Scholarship, treasurer, Member Scholarship & Gold Committees; Nicole Piggott, vice-president, chair BASF Strategic Planning.

Since its inception in 1981, the BASF has devoted a great deal of effort to ensuring that their objectives of supporting Black learners and elevating the Black community are met. By networking with other organizations, they have been able to contribute over three hundred scholarships to meritorious students at the undergraduate and graduate levels.

Every year during the month of September, BASF awards eight to ten scholarships to Black students at the CEGEP, undergraduate, and graduate levels. Amongst the organizations that the BASF collaborates with are the Batshaw Youth and Family Centres and

Foundation, in support of the Batshaw-BASF Excellence Award for Youth and the Black Studies Center Charity Scholarship Fund. The Batshaw Youth and Family Centres and Foundation helps English-speaking and Jewish communities in Montreal in cases of child abuse, serious youth behavioural problems, child neglect, and abandonment. Some of the services Batshaw offers such as tutoring, cultural and sports activities, and therapy, align with the BASF's goals. The foundation also offers activities that help build leadership skills and confidence, as well as scholarships for job training and higher education.

BASF's collaboration with the Batshaw Youth and Family Centres is the result of the efforts of BASF's former president Mrs. Sylvia Piggott. This scholarship of $1000 offered yearly since 2012 is given to a post-secondary student who has received or is an applicant for the Lois Daly Scholarship, which is offered to youth who are receiving or have received services from Batshaw. The recipient must also identify as a member of the Black community.

BASF's collaboration with the Black Studies Center has resulted, since September 2019, in a renewable $2,500 scholarship given to a student taking part in community development studies.

For Sylvia Piggott, the results of BASF's efforts demonstrated how for Black students to succeed, they need support from parents, governments, and community organizations. Though support from parents and community organizations is present, it continues to be lacking on a provincial and municipal level. To better support the Black youth in higher education, Piggott suggested that municipal and provincial governments need to provide sufficient funding.

In addition to scholarships and strong network building, the BASF also offers diverse activities to its clients such as career counselling and advice, and it also organizes an annual golf tournament to raise funds. Titled the Jackie Robinson International Golf Tournament—in honour of Montreal Royals baseball club star Jackie Robinson—it attracts professionals and past recipients of BASF scholarships who wish to give back.

Table de Concertation and Mathieu Da Costa Foundation 1991

The Table de Concertation of 1991 was the result of efforts by a group of activists and organizations from the English-speaking Black community in Quebec and Montreal, who met with the provincial government and the city of Montreal in 1990 and 1991 to demand that they recognize the existence and contributions of Black people in Quebec and Montreal. These activists and community organizers also requested that the government work with the Black community to come up with a plan that would ensure the social and economic improvement of Blacks in Quebec.

Negotiations and representations by the Black community were held with the city in 1990. They included the QBBE, the Jamaican Association, the BCCQ, the Black Coalition of Quebec, and the Afro-Canadian. In addition, a meeting took place with Premier Robert Bourassa on May 19th, 1992.

From these consultations, the Table de Concertation for the English-speaking Black Community was born.

The goal of this Table de Concertation was to develop the English-speaking Black community in Montreal with the provincial government's input. A number of committees met on a regular basis. Among them were committees on youth education, arts and culture, and community and economic development. It was also at this Table de Concertation that the Montreal Association of Black Businesspersons and Professionals proposed the creation of the Mathieu Da Costa Foundation. This project was also supported by the network of community tables de concertation and other organizations present.

For a number of years, the Mathieu Da Costa Foundation showcased and promoted Black-owned businesses and provided them with financial support for workshops and conferences, an example of which being the Salon Économique Mathieu Da Costa on March 21st, 1997. The foundation has continued to be impactful, and experiences gained from it have been used to set up the Black Entrepreneurship Fund with the provincial government. The deliberations between the city of Montreal and the Black activists also led to the city agreeing to declare February Black History Month in Montreal.

BBCQ/BCA and Val Morin Meeting (Creation of the Black Community Forum) 1992

The Val Morin Community Forum is another project that stemmed from the Table de Concertation for the English-speaking Black Community of 1991–92. This forum was established to include and engage the broader Black community in policy initiatives that were discussed at the Table de Concertation, and in response to issues of concern to the Black community such as education, youth employment, and justice. Moreover, since Black people in Montreal come from diverse backgrounds and belong to different community organizations, the forum was supposed to help the community overcome its differences, to offer unified representation when dealing with the three different levels of the government. For Leith Hamilton and Dr. Clarence Bayne, it was also important that "a systematic and more holistic approach" be adopted to resolve issues within the community, and ways to do this would be decided on at the forum.

These efforts to create a united front for the betterment of the Black community led to the principles and operation protocols that Dr. Leo Bertley prepared for the forum. The fact that the community also got the provincial government to agree to hold these meetings on an ongoing basis is further proof that the united strategy was a success.

In preparation for the forum, two independent researchers were hired by the Black Community Council of Quebec administration, the main organizers of the event. The agenda and the themes of the event were set by the founding members of the BCCQ Federation, namely the Black Theatre Workshop, the Quebec Board of Black Educators, the Montreal Association of Black Businesspersons and Professionals, and the Black Studies Center. Since the forum was not an organization and hence did not have a charter, its governing power came from the Black community organizations it represented. In Mr. Leith Hamilton's address to the forum on July 5th, 1992 he explained that,

The vision for the community is that of unity and is not just one of a small handful of people working towards the goal. There is a need to develop an internal agenda in the community that leads to strength and not weakness. We must look at specific things that strengthen and reinforce community structures. The ultimate goal is to get more resources into the community. We must determine how we can help organizations use the funding effectively once they do receive their resources.

The federal minister of Multiculturalism and Citizenship, with the support of the Quebec minister of Cultural Communities and the city of Montreal, funded the forum, which took place in July 1992. The Val Morin Black Community Report of 1992 states that the main purpose of the forum was the following:

1. To develop a process which will identify a long-term development plan for the Black Community

2. To ensure that this planning process is a cooperative effort within the Black community

3. To identify and promote a structure to support the planning process

4. To develop effective partnerships within the network of Black community groups and to encourage effective implementation strategies for the benefit of the total community

5. To provide a Forum for networking and strengthening existing relationships

Revisions of purposes two, three and five were proposed at the 2016 forum:

2. To ensure that this planning process is cooperative and collaborative

3. To encourage and promote the development of strategic partnerships and networks that benefit the Black community and the larger society

5. To provide a network for communication, the transfer of knowledge and information; and to facilitate the general expansion of ingenuity (i.e., capacity for innovation and problem solving) and social capital

The forum consisted of workshops and discussions that identified the most pressing issues and needs within the Quebec Black community. Once these were identified, "an ad hoc community committee chaired by specialists and professionals from the Black community" was created.

Throughout the forum the most pressing issue was the chronic unemployment of Black youth and their overrepresentation in the criminal justice system. To resolve this, the forum developed a tactical plan that would ensure Black youths were supported and provided with tools for appropriate education and training. This issue was later taken to a May 19th, 1992 meeting with Premier Bourassa and addressed again by Dr. Bayne in a memo sent to the Honourable Sheila Finestone by Rick Gill in response to her Call to Address Issues of Training for Youth in Our Community on July 5th, 1994.

In response to the Black community's concern about youth education, the Honourable Sheila Finestone put forward a plan for social collaboration between traditional service providers in Metropolitan Montreal and Black community representatives and organizations. This collaboration's main goal was to adopt a holistic approach to resolve issues facing English-speaking Black youths between the ages of eighteen and twenty-five. The collaboration had the Honourable Sheila Finestone's full support, and she advocated for it within the Liberal Party in Ottawa.

The discussions held and recommendations made during the Val Morin Black Forum led to many historic events and organizations that we still have in Montreal today, an example being the Black Community Resource Centre.

BCRC

The Black Community Resource Centre (BCRC) originated from the 1992 Val Morin Black Forum, where it was determined that the BCRC would be the Secretariat of the Black Community Forum, with a permanent administrative structure. To establish the BCRC, the Black Studies Center, Quebec Board of Educators, Montreal Association for Black Businesspersons and Professionals, and the Black Theatre Workshop, together with the Côte-des-Neiges Black Community Association and Jamaica Association, held meetings on a regular basis and organized workshops on strategic planning. These meetings led to the eventual creation of the BCRC with funding from the federal government. From the beginning, the BCRC's main mandate has been to offer

"Innovative support services" to the Black community, whether to individuals or sister organizations.

The BCRC runs a number of projects that raise awareness regarding education, justice, and health as they pertain to the Black community. For example, during the Covid pandemic, a significant amount of effort was put toward educating the English-speaking community on how they could protect themselves, with information sessions on the Covid vaccine provided by health professionals. There are also dental care information sessions that are held in collaboration with students from McGill University. In recent years, it has run the Book Project, Black in Quebec program, Intergenerational Health and Social Program, Project Woke, and other initiatives.

The Creation of Black History Month Festivities and Round Table

Though it was not until January 28th, 1992 that the Montreal City Council officially declared February as Black History Month, English-speaking Black people in the city of Montreal had been celebrating it starting in the 1960s. For example, every February members of the Negro Community Centre (NCC) would organize events for Black History Week. Moreover, Black university student groups from Concordia and McGill also took initiatives to teach people about the importance of Black history throughout the month of February.

By 1990, Black community groups wished to see Black history and the contributions of Blacks in Quebec and Montreal celebrated by everyone. They created a coalition of Black community groups and activists who then persuaded the Quebec Human Rights Commission to support their request for Black History Month recognition. The Human Rights Commission agreed and provided funding for the celebrations. The coalition then lobbied the city to do the same. Mayor Jean Doré agreed and made it his mission to ensure that Black History Month was recognized in Montreal in February of 1991. February was officially declared Black History Month by the city council the next year, and to organize and coordinate activities, a Roundtable for Black History Month was created.

Canadian Association of Black Lawyers

The Canadian Association of Black Lawyers (CABL) is a national organization of legal professionals. Its main goals are to create a network and give back to the Black community in Canada. The founders drew inspiration from an international event organized by the National Bar Association (NBA), the US organization of African-American attorneys and judges in 1994 in Toronto. At this time, the organization was led by Paulette Brown, who in 2015 would become the first woman of colour and third African-American president of the American Bar Association. After holding discussions throughout 1995 with members of the Black bar in Canada and NBA representatives, the Canadian association was created and incorporated as a not-for-profit organization a year later. Amongst the founding members of the organization are Roger Rowe, Winston Mattis, Patricia Deguire, Lynda Searles, David Mercury, Sonja Salmon, and Chris Wilson.

To accomplish their goal of giving back, the organization has participated in many initiatives. Between 1996 and 1997, the CABL collaborated with the University of Toronto Law Class of 1990, to create a scholarship award in honour of Michael Kelly for second- and third- year Black law students attending University of Toronto. CABL members also offered mentorship to high school students who are members of visible minorities through the University of Toronto's mentorship program. Members were able to build a network through their participation in the landmark case of O'Keefe v. Loewen Group, where the plaintiff was awarded $500 million in damages.

The CABL continues to provide a supportive network to young Black lawyers, especially those just starting their careers, through its Young Lawyers Division. The CABL has chapters in Toronto, Alberta, British Columbia, Nova Scotia, Ottawa, and Quebec.

Quebec's Black Medical Association

The Quebec Black Medical Association was created by Dr. Elrie Tucker in the 1990s. Dr. Tucker of Trinidad had moved to Montreal to complete his studies in medicine at McGill University in the 1950s. Despite graduating in the top ten students in his class, Dr. Tucker often faced discrimination. He was told to go back to his country when trying to find work in Montreal in the 1950s.

He went on to become Royal Victoria Hospital's first Black obstetrician in 1967 and opened his own birthing centre. With his friend Dr. Stan Blicker, Dr. Tucker also opened a mammography and thermography clinic. Having experienced it first hand, Dr. Tucker was aware of the amount of racism that Black youths trying to go into the field of medicine faced. He also knew that only a very small number of Black kids ever got accepted into medical school or received scholarships to complete their studies. This motivated him to start the Quebec Black Medical Association in 1991. Through this association he was able to single-handedly raise funds for over five hundred scholarships for Black youths who wanted to study medicine.

Today, the Quebec Black Medical Association continues to build on Dr. Tucker's legacy by funding projects to promote and contribute to public education of the medical sciences; to enhance the quality of public, medical, and social services provided to disadvantaged persons; and fund grants for Black students who have demonstrated leadership, academic achievement, or community involvement, helping them pursue studies in the medical sciences.

Conclusion

In order to respond to the challenges they faced from 1980–2000, Black Montrealers came together and organized. They created community organizations, educational funds, social groups, and events that elevated Black people and their culture. They held roundtable discussions in the early 1990s with the intent of creating Black-led community initiatives that would serve the communities' various needs. They also organized conferences and tables de concertation. These accomplishments were the result of Black Montreal activists and community organizers coming together and demanding policy from the city, the province, and the federal government. Further, the 1990s saw Black legal and medical professional associations emerge in Montreal.

Conclusion: A Continuum of Resistance

Fanta Ly

The persistent Black mobilization, locally, nationally, and internationally, propelled discussions on the pervasiveness of anti-Black racism to the forefront of societal debates. This mainstreaming, while reflective of an increasing recognition of the insidious nature of racism, has not been accepted by all in Quebec. Discussions about the state of racial injustice have been met with denial and most troublingly re-affirmed at the highest level of the state by Premier François Legault. However, it is not lost on Black Montrealers, that the state and its institution perpetuating, legitimizing, and contributing to the maintenance of anti-Black racism, has denied the existence of systemic racism. This notwithstanding, systemic racism is a fact of Black life globally.

In her seminal work *Lose Your Mother: A Journey Along the Atlantic Slave Route,* Saidiya Hartman coins the "afterlives of slavery" to illustrate how contemporary Black life is still embedded and shaped by the same ideologies and systems that have historically justified violence and undermined Black livelihoods. As such, amid the 2020 heightened collective consciousness meant to be attuned to race relations, the hope and aim were that the material reality and livelihood of Black Montrealers stop mirroring the "afterlives of slavery."

In this conclusion to *Where They Stood*, I discuss some of its manifestations through practices, policies, behaviours, laws, and discourses that have nurtured and maintained anti-Black racism. I turn to domains and incidents including state responses to address systemic racism, police brutality, discrimination in the education system, and advocacy initiatives. While attentive to institutional challenges that undergird anti-Black racism, my analysis unmasks the trauma and pain, but centres on the persistence of Black communities that have always demanded better for themselves and the generations that will follow. To that end, I examine how Black Montrealers have embraced Black traditions mobilizing and seeking out local and international solidarity in the face of limited and often antagonistic state intervention.

Systemic Discrimination in Quebec: A False Canadian Exceptionalism?

To discuss the ways in which anti-Black racism and systemic discrimination have impacted the livelihood of Black Montrealers, it is necessary to define the concept, and contextualize why it has become a polemic term and subject in Quebec, and not in other parts of Canada. This section aims to highlight that despite regional dynamics unique to Quebec shaping discussions on anti-Black racism and systemic racism more broadly, there is value in taking a step back from generalizations on what is commonly referred to as Quebec's particular brand of racism to distinguish state discourses and practices. A careful analysis reveals that while the political discourse is different in Quebec, the practices of state violence, harm, and disregard shown towards Black Quebecers and Black Canadians remain identical, albeit more sophisticated at certain levels.

Discussions on systemic racism in Quebec took an unexpected and very important place in Quebec public debates in 2020 amid the purported global reckoning on anti-Black racism on the global stage. This period referred to as the "dual pandemic of COVID-19 and anti-Black racism" shows the plight that often shaped Black life as the disproportionate mortality rate of Black populations skyrocketed during the pandemic. These realities impelled and generated an unprecedented level of care and discussions on inequality, racial trauma, and the systemic nature of these disadvantages in the mainstream media.

In this context, the focus on Black life was met by white backlash whereby white individuals respond negatively and at times viscerally to racial progress or opportunities for racial progress. This manifested itself in opposition to the use and recognition of systemic racism as it related to Black life in Quebec. Yet, the Quebec Human Rights Commission had long ascertained the presence of systemic racism in Quebec drawing on a longstanding definition of the Ontario Human Rights Commission. This definition referred to systemic racism "as patterns of behaviour, policies or practices that are part of the structures of an organization, and which create or perpetuate disadvantage for racialized persons." In August 2021, the Quebec Human Rights Commission issued a reflective document on the notion of systemic racism, restating its presence and its relevance to Human Rights legislation and bodies.

Amid the immediate backlash and debate in 2020, Premier Legault convened a task force on racism chaired by two Black Ministers—Lionel Carmant and Nadine Girault—a move that some decried as tokenistic given that the mandate of the task force explicitly left out systemic racism. The chairs reaffirmed the government's position that discrimination existed but its definition was undecided and subject to debate, and therefore did not warrant additional debates. In the final report of the task force, both Black Ministers discussed their own personal experiences with racism. The approach reflects a common strategy to deflect from shift systemic issues by reflecting on individuals. While systemic issues are the sum of individual experiences, they shared their experiences in a way that did not allow for connection to broader and systemic issues. This Black Ministerial intervention also showcased the ways in which race, class, and social capital shaped Where Influential Black Politicians in Quebec Stood.

A necessary acknowledgment of the intersectional and at times diverging interest of Black Montrealers made hypervisible due to white decision-makers attempting to justify their decisions by putting the few Black officials at the forefront. Ultimately, such platforming is instrumentalized to lend credence to government discourse and action. This is a common strategy that will be revisited when discussing educational reforms under the banner of Equity, Diversity, and Inclusion in Higher Education.

The instrumentalization of a long-established term did not cause much controversy in the rest of Canada.

Nonetheless, it would be erroneous to frame the debate on systemic racism as unique to the Quebec political landscape. At the Federal level, Brenda Lucki, Commissioner of the Royal Canadian Mounted Police, was one of few high-profile public servants who initially denied the existence of systemic racism within her force only to backtrack amid outcry and ridicule. Such intervention from officials across the country captured the willful ignorance and at times genuine ignorance of systemic racism. What is interesting is the response. In most of Canada, attempts to deny long-affirmed and recognized systemic issues were not ridiculed, whereas the Quebec response fuelled a political debate.

Another potential explanation for the disparate response at the federal level is that such debates took place against the backdrop of the United Nations Decade for People for African Descent—proclaimed in December 2013 and set from 2015 to 2024 through a resolution of the United Nations General Assembly. Although the federal government of Canada only recognized the decade in 2018, its commitment is reflected in Ministerial mandate letters and budgetary allocations to the thematic program centres Recognition, Justice, and Development. Urging governments across the globe to examine and improve the livelihoods of People of African Descent in their respective countries, these made any denial of systemic racism ludicrous both domestically and internationally, considering this commitment was embedded within its international obligations.

While there is a clear difference between the federal and provincial levels in recognizing systemic racism at the discursive level, government action does not show much difference. During the summer of mobilization 2020, Justin Trudeau took part in the protest and took a knee and raised his fist in solidarity. As with François Legault's statement on racism, he did so alongside two Black officials, which included Minister Ahmed Hussain and Member of Parliament Greg Fergus. This performance and representational politics is a key feature of Canadian racism, and in some quarters serves to elucidate any potential accusations of racism.

Similarly, at the federal level, the government's engagement with Black communities often reflected what Eli Kamno referenced in his song *Démocratie*:

> "*Parce que la <u>main qui DONNE</u> c'est la <u>main qui TUE</u>, mais aussi la <u>main qui DIRIGE</u>*"

> — "Because the hand that GIVES is the hand that KILLS, but also the hand that DIRECTS."

The government championing inclusion is the very same one being sued as part of the Black Class Action—the largest employment-law class action for the practice of Black Employee Exclusion—and seeking to have the case thrown out.

This case is particularly interesting as it reveals troubling patterns of anti-Black racism within the Canadian Human Rights Commission, the agency normally tasked to investigate such complaints. In comparison, as will be later discussed the Quebec Human Rights Commission has been complicit in its mishandling of racial discrimination cases and its overall poor functioning due to deliberate underfunding. Such matters are identical in that the human rights body is failing

Black Canadians and Black Quebecers at the federal and provincial levels.

Another helpful reference highlighting that political recognition of systemic racism has little to no bearing on engagement and commitment to Black livelihoods is reflected in Montreal Mayor Valérie Plante's. management of the police budget through her party Projet Montreal. While she has unequivocally acknowledged systemic racism and its impact on Black communities, she has repeatedly recommitted to increasing the police budget to astronomical sums amid persistent racial profiling. Police brutality and calls to Defund the Police. While officials at all levels have been inconsistent or shown their support for Black lives performatively, Black Montrealers have relied on their own consistent and novel efforts to advance their rights.

From Mobilization to Litigation: The Creation of Black-led Legal Clinics and Advocacy Organizations

The coalescence of various Black community organizations advocating for equal treatment has paved the way for the creation of legal clinics. Among these are the Clinique juridique Saint-Michel, founded by criminalist Fernando Belton, and the Clinique juridique de Montréal Nord, founded by Marie-Livia Beaugé.

These clinics fill an important gap in access to justice by providing information to individuals considering legal remedies. However, these clinics do not have the capacity to provide representation. As such, individuals confronted with a legal issue can seek out assistance to identify the legal issue and outline their options. However, any action must be handled on its own through formal representation. For those who rely on their services, being informed of your rights does not lead to having your case addressed.

A notable and recent exception to the limited scope of services is the creation of a racial profiling committee at the Clinique juridique Saint-Michel. This new committee offers its users full representation in bringing cases to the Quebec Human Rights Commission and the Police Ethics Commission, amongst other bodies. Compared to past efforts, the Clinique juridique Saint-Michel constitutes a pivotal shift in access to justice, ensuring that individuals can retain a lawyer.

Before the establishment of these clinics, the Centre for Research Action on Race Relations, led by Fo Niemi, was the primary community organization supporting Black litigants in matters of racial discrimination, profiling, or any human rights violations. These legal procedures can be retraumatizing, with cases denouncing violence themselves becoming further violent encounters with police and the courts. The growing number of self-represented litigants should be seen as a necessary path toward access to justice as many often underestimate the complexity and the moral and psychological support when undertaking such lengthy and difficult cases. Indeed, many Black women filing cases of police violence have been met with reprisal, and after filing a complaint have been the subject of made-up charges of obstruction of justice. This type of retaliatory tactic is meant to dissuade, discourage, and exhaust the potential complainant.

In 2014, when Majiza Philip filed a complaint after having her arm broken by a Montreal police officer, she was charged with obstruction of justice. At trial, the judge dismissed the charge against Ms. Philip and found that the application of an obstruction of justice charge "cast[ed] doubt on the officers' version of events in the 2017 trial."

After undergoing surgery, she still has a scar from the incident and noted that "'Every day I see a six-inch scar on my arm, and I think about it." This powerful testimony captures both visible and invisible scars Black Montrealers continue to face. Moreover, in this case, she sought $700,000 but was given a $95,000 settlement in 2022, eight years after the violent incident occurred. The adage that "justice delayed is justice denied" applies to the awarding of damages in this case, and the thousands of cases that take an unreasonable amount of time to be heard. Such delays are caused by the understaffing and under-resourcing of the Quebec Human Rights Commission. To be clear, this is a deliberate choice and a strategy that reflects the lack of government care regarding funding what should be of the premier human rights body. Such shortcomings have inspired Black Montrealers to set up their own initiatives and scale their existing Rights programming.

The emergence of organizations that share similar mandates has not been met with rivalry but with cooperation and collaboration. The magnitude of the issues, and the number of underserviced community members, means that initiatives lessen the burden on existing organizations. This collaborative model is underpinned by Black solidarity and reflected in the programming of these organizations through initiatives such as Know Your Rights campaigns and car rallies against racial profiling. One of the most notable initiatives pertained to legal resources.

In 2020, the DESTA Black Youth Network established the Black Legal Action Fund with a mandate to "pay for the legal expenses of those with demonstrably legitimate cases of appeal. The legitimacy of a case will be determined from a holistic approach. The fund will also go towards supporting those coming out of incarceration, to help them re-integrate into society." This support is vital,l as access to lawyers and legal information is a major hurdle that the mobilization of resources can address. But representation alone does not offer individuals who have faced racism and intersecting forms of discrimination a guaranteed remedy. The very institutions tasked with redressing discrimination are also marred,and have replicated the very discrimination they have been mandated to redress, thereby putting a significant strain on complainants. It can take over three years, for example, for a complaint to go through the commission process. In addition, the commission has often been criticized for neglecting to look into the systemic issues and the intersecting grounds of discrimination at play. This failure has led many to seek remedies transnationally.

An example is the case of Marie Ismé and her son, who has autism, and who has been denied access to special education. Despite significant media coverage, this situation was not resolved; a complaint taken to the United Nations Committee on the Rights of the Child later found that systemic racism was embedded in that complaint process.

The differential treatment experienced by Black students and students with disabilities continues to undermine educational attainment in a province with the lowest high-school graduation rate in Canada. The impact of anti-Black racism on the morale and prospects of Black students remains a cause for concern. In a 2022 study by Statistics Canada titled Black History Month by the Numbers, it was revealed that a 2016 survey noted: "although 94% of Black youth aged 15 to 25 said that they would like to get a bachelor's degree or higher, 60% thought that they could." These numbers show the impact of the ostracization and exclusion of Black students when it comes to benefiting from a learning environment that will propel them into the next stage of their academic and professional lives.

Organizations such as the Centre for Research Action on Race Relations have had to resort to international human rights bodies to denounce the mistreatment and the failure of domestic remedies such as the Quebec Human Rights Commission addressing and redressing anti-Black racism. As Montrealers continue to push internationally, they have continued to expand their local engagements.

Montreal's Consultation on Systemic Racism
In addition to the creation of new organizations and funds to support racial discrimination litigation, Black Montrealers have also opted for innovative legal recourses through existing mechanisms such as the Public Consultation on Systemic Racism led by Balarama Holness.

Founder of a political advocacy group called Montréal en Action, Holness made use of the *By-law concerning the Montreal Charter of Rights and Responsibilities and the*

Right of Initiative (05-056) of Montreal's charter—which mandates City Council to "convene public consultations on an issue brought to it by a petition containing at least fifteen thousand signatures. "Holness and his group canvassed and collected a total of 20,000 signatures, going above the required amount for immediate use: "Under the right of initiative, a public consultation on systemic racism and discrimination." On July 27, 2018, they presented a 22,000-signature petition, and a consultation led by the Office de consultation publique de Montréal (OCPM) took place on August 29, 2018 and December 4, 2019, with testimonies from over seven thousand people.

The report that followed highlighted the pervasiveness of systemic racism in Montreal, and the recommendations led to the establishment of Montreal's first Commissioner on systemic racism. While this position was welcomed, the nomination of Bochra Manaï to the role caused significant controversy; the reasons for this ranged from negating the need for this role to complaints that this position was a partisan one. For Black Montrealers, the consultation and the position came from the labour of mobilized Black citizens who were once again overlooked and excluded from an institution they had not only laid the foundation for but successfully built.

The Continuing Legacy of the Sir George Williams Affair and the Tradition of Zealous Advocacy in the Academy

The education system in Quebec has remained a site of contestation where Black students and faculty continue to carve out a place for themselves. The 2020 uprising following the murder of George Floyd led to wide-ranging commitments across the university sector, including the implementation of an Action Plan to Address Anti-Black Racism at McGill and a Taskforce and the establishment of a Black Perspectives Office at Concordia. The concomitant energy, zeal, and despair that underpinned the Sir George Williams Affair continue to shape the advocacy initiatives of Black students. In this section, I will discuss institutional changes suppressed by the 2020 mobilization at Concordia and McGill and situate these initiatives within similar calls for reforms in higher education both nationally and internationally.

On June 30, 2020, McGill University's principal, Suzanne Fortier, announced an array of institutional reforms to address anti-Black racism, joining myriad university administrators doing the same. As McGill was also preparing to celebrate its bicentennial, the university announced the creation of an Anti-Black Racism Action Plan, with a release date set for September 20, 2020. This plan had the potential to bring about needed change at a time when the institution was looking inward. However, the interests of white administrators remained at the centre of McGill's plans. Principal Fortier appointed a white man—Provost and Vice-Principal (Academic) Christopher Manfredi—to lead the initiative. This decision raised doubts from the outset about the plan's potential. Such doubts were grounded in legitimate concerns about the Provost's expertise and the institutional locus. After all, why would someone with no expertise or experience or proximity to McGill's Black history and community be appointed to this position?

Beyond the individual, this appointment was an anomaly institutionally, as well. One of the main criticisms pertained to the academic mandate and thus the scope of the plan. Why would a McGill-wide plan be vested in an office that does not have McGill-wide jurisdiction? Similarly, while Black staff was hired as equity, diversity, and inclusion advisers under the plan, they all reported to white administrators and were operating with very detailed mandates.

One key aspect of these appointments is the continued pushback against Black student advocacy and support. For example, the position of Black Student Liaison Officer meant to guide, advise, and support students have been expressly mandated not to advocate for students. The newly-created position of Associate Dean of Black and Indigenous Flourishing at the Faculty of Law was similarly restricted, even though the ethos of the position was meant to offer student support. This position was hastily terminated after one year, and many other staff hired under the plan—including the Local Wellness Advisor for BIPOC Students—left their roles in the absence of adequate support. The departure of staff meant to support Black students for reasons similar to those that led to their hiring attests to resistance from senior administrators to bring about genuine change and engage authentically.

These flawed institutional reforms often branded as progressive and innovative have allowed universities to bury and avoid accountability. The backtrack of needed and impactful student support mirrors the experience shared by Brenda Paris—a leader within Montreal's Black community and a former staff member in Dawson

College's Black and Third World Studies Department—who recounted the creation and subsequent disembedding of this Department that reveals further resistance to the institutionalization of support for Black and racialized students across higher education. This history is essential to understand the patterns of institutional apathy and efforts toward the educational attainment of Black and racialized students. Further, understanding these decorative initiatives can also inform mobilization and advocacy strategies of Black student groups at this critical juncture of purported institutional awakening.

The rollout of anti-Black racism initiatives at Concordia University took a significantly more meaningful and structural approach. Rather than a superficial and expediently developed action plan, a task force was convened and conducted extensive consultations before the issuance of a report. In the interim, institutional support was offered to Concordia's Black community through the creation of the Black Perspectives Office, which also holds an advocacy mandate. One of the most meaningful outcomes of this process was the long-awaited institutional apology for the Sir George Williams Affairs. While the response was overwhelmingly positive, important questions arose on the absence of reparations.

For How Long? Black Existence Still Requires Resistance

This selective overview of the varying manifestations of anti-Black racism through discourse, policies, and legal structures highlights the array of violent encounters—institutional or physical—that continue to impact the daily lives of Black Montrealers. The theme of the UN Decade centering Recognition, Justice, and Development is fitting, capturing Where Black Montrealers Have Always Stood in their relentless pursuit of equality through accountability, their strategic efforts to coalesce and develop new organizations apt for their advocacy needs, and to ensure that recognition shifts from an ask to one that is acquired.

After all, Black Montrealers knew Where They Stood long before George Floyd was murdered. Black Montrealers knew Where They Stood before their livelihoods became a hashtag. Black Montrealers have unapologetically shown Where They Stood, And, most importantly Black Montrealers have taken stock of Who Stood By Their Side. The remaining question is How Much Longer Will They Need to Stand?

Organization Guide

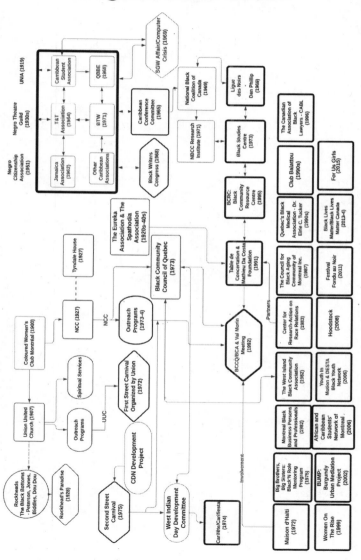

Organizational Guide Key

Organization

Initiative and or group

Event

Important figures

Created or inspired by

Linked

External Linked Events (1970-)

Concordia (JMSB) collaborates w/ Black community orgs. in business start up training - the creation of ICED (1989-1992)	Yolande James Task Force & establishment of the Black Entrepreneurship Fund by the Gov. of Quebec (2005-6)	Honorable Mention: Ballerama runs for mayor (2021)
The emergence of the Institute for Development Community Minority Entrepreneurs (1989-1992)	The creation of Black History Month Festivities and Round Table (1992-3)	Resurgence of BLM movements across North America - George Floyd, Breonna Taylor, etc. (2020)
Montreal International Jazz Festival (1980)	Creation of the Black Academic Scholarship Fund (1991)	Murder of Trayvon Martin (2012)
The October Crisis (1970)	Festival International Nuits d'Afrique (1990)	Murder of Freddy Villeneuva (2008)

For Further Reading

Austin, David. *Fear of a Black Nation: Race, Sex and Security in Sixties Montreal*. Toronto: Between the Lines, 2013; 2nd edition 2023.

Farmer, Bonnie and Marie Lafrance. *Oscar Lives Next Door: A Story Inspired by Oscar Peterson's Childhood*. Toronto: Owlkids, 2015.

Gilmore, John. *Swinging in Paradise: The Story of Jazz in Montreal*. Montreal: Véhicule Press, 1988.

High, Steven. *Deindustrializing Montreal: Entangled Histories of Race, Residence, and Class*. Montreal and Kingston: McGill-Queen's University Press, 2022.

Maynard, Robin. *Policing Black Lives: State Violence in Canada from Slavery to the Present*. Black Point, Nova Scotia: Fernwood Publishing, 2017.

Cummings, Ronald and Nalini Mohabir, eds. *The Fire That Time: Transnational Black Radicalism and the Sir George Williams Occupation*. Montreal: Black Rose Books, 2022.

Sarsfield, Mairuth. *No Crystal Stair*. Original ed.: Vancouver: Stoddart, 1997. Rpt. Montreal: Linda Leith Publishing, 2022.

Kelley, Ninette and Michael Trebilcock. *The Making of the Mosaic: A History of Canadian Immigration Policy*, 2nd ed. Toronto: University of Toronto Press, 2010.

Williams, Dorothy W. *Blacks in Montreal, 1628-1986: An Urban Demography.* Original ed.: Cowansville, QC: Éditions Yvon Blais, 1989. Rpt. Montreal: D. W Williams, 2008.

Williams, Dorothy W. *The Road to Now: A History of Blacks in Montreal.* Montreal: Véhicule Press, 1998.

Biographical Notes on Authors and Supporters

Sara DeMelo-Zare is a Concordia University alumna with a deep passion for local histories and activism. She hopes this book will help educate our students and preserve the memories of the important individuals who helped make our city what it is today. As the Project Coordinator, Sara was involved in the planning, editing, and writing of the work, as well as penning parts herself. Sara and her colleague Ayana conducted outreach, organized in-school workshops, worked one-on-one with authors through the writing process, and compiled the anthology.

Ayana Monuma is located in Tio'tiá:ke (Montreal). As the Youth Animator of the project, she worked closely with each youth, supporting them through their journey to authorship. She aspires to continue working for the Black communities of Montreal and make room for the often silenced and ignored Black voices.

Raeanne Francis (MSc) is the Managing Director of the Black Community Resource Centre (BCRC). In her role, she works to develop and implement English-speaking programs in health, access to justice, socio-cultural development, education, employment, and economic development to improve the well-being of Black and other minority communities in the Quebec and Canadian landscapes. She worked alongside Dr. Clarence Bayne on managing this project from conceptualization to publication.

Desirée Rochat is a post-doctoral fellow in the Department of History at the University of Toronto. Her knowledge and experience in the community sector helped guide the project staff in completing the book.

Matthew "Zack" Mullone is a Creole-Texan anthropologist and artist. He joined this project to tell the stories of those underrepresented in the traditional Black history narrative. He also wanted to learn more about Montreal's Black history, and how it might connect to that of the United States. His chapter discusses the jazz movement, porters and the railway economy, migration, and the role of Black women in community organizing.

Sherwins Jean is a recent graduate of the BA History program at Concordia University, looking to pursue continued education in archival preservation. She is of Haitian descent and has always felt as though her community was better accepted in Montreal due to their attachment to the French-speaking world. Jean wanted to shine a light on the wildly underappreciated English-speaking Black community and its contributions to our rich cultural landscape. Her chapter discusses the First World War and military segregation, Marcus Garvey's Pan-Africanist ideology, and the United Negro Improvement Association (UNIA).

Anne Victoria Jean-François is a Haitian-Canadian singer and writer. She was born in Montreal and raised in Calgary and returned to the city to pursue a communications degree at Concordia. Jean-François was always intrigued by storytelling and was motivated to join the *Where They Stood* project to elevate the voices of those who paved the way for her to thrive. Her chapter focuses on the Prohibition era and organized crime traveling from the United States into Montreal, and how they both influenced Montreal's Black community. She tapped into how music and song shaped the community as well.

Jessica Williams-Daley is a first year McGill University student Majoring in Psychology with a Double Minor in Behavioural Sciences and Anthropology. Since childhood, she has always showcased a profound connection to the brain, emotions and social interactions and utilized this gift to provide emotional support to others through her psychological teachings. Delving into prominent psychological, medical and sociological research at the young age of twelve, she discovered how the perpetual cycle of discrimination, inequality, and injustices (evolving into transgenerational trauma) in the Black community negatively impacted them in various domains and gravely disproportionately in the health and wellness sector. Jessica hopes to shed light on this through this project by informing readers of the silenced stories of Black Montrealers that have shaped the city's cultural landscape and history. Her section discusses the 1940s, spanning from Black enlistment in the Royal Canadian Air Force to Black musical milestones.

Renee White, is a Canadian-Jamaican born and raised in Montreal. She believes that understanding the struggles of those before us helps unite us. This project allowed her to feel more connected to her community, knowing how far they have come despite various challenges. Her chapter covers the 1950s, a time of early immigration which gave rise to the Negro Citizenship Association

(NCA). It also explores Montreal's popular jazz artists and nightclubs and their influence in the city.

Amanda Asomani-Nyarko, also known as GG is a 24-year-old writer, poet, and spoken-word artist of Jamaican and Ghanaian descent, born and raised in Montreal. She is a recent graduate of Concordia University with a Bachelor of Arts in English Literature, and is currently enrolled at McGill University studying for a postgraduate diploma in Public Relations and Communications Management. Amanda participated in this project to share the stories of Black immigrants who came to Montreal, whose contributions have oftentimes been overlooked. Her chapter explores the various societal shifts occurring in Montreal during the 1960s that later influenced the creation and evolution of Black spaces.

Yoanna Joseph is an emerging singer, poet, and playwright from Tiotia:ke/Montreal. She has an undergraduate degree in French literature, and storytelling is one of her absolute greatest passions. As a second-generation immigrant, she always wanted to know more about the history of Black Canadians, particularly because she didn't learn any of it in school and felt that Where They Stood would help her learn about the history of Canada and also pay tribute to the Afro-Canadians who came before her. As a child, she dreamed of elevating Black stories and voices through her art while creating dialog around other subjects and topics that are close to her heart, like discrimination, and now she's doing just that.

Donna Fabiola Ingabire graduated from Concordia University with a double major in community, public affairs, and policy studies & political science. Ingabire spent the majority of her childhood in Eastern and

Southern Africa, and finally settled in Montreal in 2008. Her background in policy has led to a keen interest in both government regulations and policy responses. As an English-speaking immigrant and Black Montrealer, the familiarity of the erasure of the contributions made by those who came before her in this city has not been shocking; what has been surprising is the extent of this erasure. Fabiola believes that by participating in this project not only is she ensuring that these contributions receive the recognition they deserve, but she is also letting future generations of Black Montrealers know that they too matter and belong here. Her chapter explores various Black community organizations and social groups created between 1980–99. Her research has focused on their histories and the needs that their founders were trying to address.

Fanta Ly is J.D. / B.C.L Candidate at McGill University's Faculty of Law. She draws on her roots hailing from the Futa Tooro (Sénégal) to the Futa Djallon (Guinea) and her multicultural upbringing spanning three continents, to reflect on African diasporic livelihoods and the theory and praxis of Black solidarity. As an aspiring lawyer, she draws on her passion for law, policy, advocacy, and community to explore the continuing strategic mobilization of Black Montrealers.

John Davids has an MA in political science and is the research coordinator at the Black Community Resource Centre. He has conducted research on Quebec's English-speaking Black community since 2020 and worked on this project in the editing phase, being a point of contact between the publishers, editors, and authors.

Melis Karayusuf was born in Izmir, Turkey. As a child she was always in love with books, arts, sculpture, and music. She trained in traditional drawing and sculpture, and then studied Computer Generated Imagery (CGI), which kickstarted her life in Canada. She believes in spreading awareness about economic inequality, and she loves learning new languages and dancing every chance she gets.

Dr. Clarence S. Bayne is a lifelong educator. With a PhD in economics from McGill, he is a professor emeritus at Concordia University's John Molson School of Business in addition to being president of the Black Community Resource Centre. Dr, Bayne, who is from Trinidad and Tobago, came to study at the University of British Columbia, then made his way to Montreal for a job, and later enrolled at McGill University. He has authored multiple peer-reviewed scientific papers and presented at national and international conferences, winning acclaim from experts around the world. Dr. Bayne's research interests are cross-disciplinary, with an emphasis on community development. Dr. Bayne made himself available to lead workshops and be interviewed by the youth. In addition, he read each draft and provided commentary.

Yvonne Sam, a native of Guyana, has combined simultaneous careers as a clinical charge nurse, nursing examiner for the Order of Nurses of Quebec, and secondary school teacher with the English Montreal School Board for over thirty years. She has multiple degrees in nursing and education. She is a regular columnist with *Montreal Community Contact* and her wide-ranging articles have appeared in the

Huffington Post, Montreal Gazette, Toronto Star, and other venues. She received the Governor General of Canada's Caring Canadian Award and is the mother of two adult sons. She researched each youth's timeframe, compiling a list of articles and topics to be referred to during the research process. She also played a significant role in connecting youths to community members.

Dr. Dorothy Abike Wills BS, MSW, MA, PhD, LLD, DHL, CM, retired as dean of the Faculty of Applied Technologies at Vanier College. She served as a member of the Immigration and Refugee Board of Canada for six years. She has taught at the high school, CEGEP, and university levels. She has served on municipal, provincial, and federal committees and has been extensively involved in Black community organizations. She has received many awards including the Order of Canada and several honorary doctorates. Dr. Wills met with each youth and provided grammar and content feedback. She talked to the youths about relevant memories and suggested significant figures to add to their research.

Together, these writers and supporters have created a wide-ranging learning tool to educate those willing to learn and provide a wider sense of belonging throughout Montreal's Black community. They hope that through education and understanding they can promote a better appreciation for the contributions of their Black predecessors.

We hope that you, the reader, will better understand and acknowledge *Where They Stood*.

A Note on Singles Essays

Where They Stood: The Evolution of the Black Anglo Community in Montreal is the most recent in a series of short Singles essays in English and in French on topics of contemporary and abiding interest.

Linda Leith Publishing | Linda Leith Éditions.

Black Community Resource Centre. **Where They Stood: The Evolution of the Black Anglo Community in Montreal.** LLP, 2023. ISBN: 9781773901343.

Boullata, Issa J. **The Bells of Memory: A Palestinian Boyhood in Jerusalem**. LLP, 2014. ISBN: 9781927535394.

Deguire, Eric. **Communication et violence. Des récits personnels à l'hégémonie américaine,** essai. LLÉ, 2020. ISBN: 9781773900605.

Delvaux, Martine. **Nan Goldin: The Warrior Medusa**, trans. David Homel. LLP, 2017. ISBN: 9781988130552.

Drimonis, Toula. **We, the Others: Allophones, Immigration, and Belonging in Canada**. LLP, 2022. ISBN: 9781773901213.

Farman, Abou. **Clerks of the Passage**. LLP, 2012. ISBN: 9780987831743.

Farman Abou. **Les lieux de passage, essais sur le mouvement et la migration,** trad. Marianne Champagne. LLÉ, 2016. ISBN : 9781988130200.

Fletcher, Raquel. **Who Belongs in Quebec? Identity Politics in a Changing Society.** LLP, 2020. ISBN: 9781927535394.

Gollner, Adam Leith. **Working in the Bathtub: Conversations with the Immortal Dany Laferrière.** LLP 2021. ISBN: 9781773900735.

Henighan, Stephen. **A Green Reef: The Impact of Climate Change.** LLP, 2013. ISBN: 9781927535271.

Jedwab, Jack. **Counterterrorism and Identities: Canadian Viewpoints.** LLP 2015. ISBN. 9781927535868.

Lavoie, Frédérick. **For Want of a Fir Tree: Ukraine Undone,** trans. Donald Winkler. LLP, 2018. ISBN: 97819881305934.

Michaud, Sara Danièle. **Scar Tissue: Tracing Motherhood,** trans. Katia Grubisic. LLP 2023. ISBN: 9781773901374.

Navarro, Pascale. **Women and Power: The Case for Parity,** trans. David Homel. LLP 2016. ISBN 9781988130156

Péan, Stanley. **Taximan,** trans. David Homel. LLP 2018. ISBN: 9781988130897.

Rowland, Wade. **Saving the CBC: Balancing and Public Service.** LLP, 2013. ISBN: 9781927535110.

Rowland, Wade. **Canada Lives Here: The Case for Public Broadcasting.** LLP 2015. ISBN: 9781927535820.

Salutin, Rick. **Keeping the Public in Public Education.** LLP, 2012. ISBN: 9780987831729.